The Mountains of Mourne

A Celebration of a Place Apart

First published in hardback in 2002

Paperback edition published in 2003 by
Appletree Press Ltd
14 Howard Street South
Belfast BT7 1AP

Tel. (0) 28 90 243074
Fax: (0) 28 90 246756
E-mail: reception@appletree.ie
Web Site: www.appletree.ie

A catalogue record for this book is available from
the British Library.

The Mountains of Mourne:
A Celebration of a Place Apart

ISBN 0-86281-872-9

Commissioning Editor: Paul Harron
Design by Stonecastle Graphics Ltd
Production: Paul McAvoy

*To Dr Arthur Mitchell, MBE, Chairman of the
Mourne Heritage Trust and lifelong campaigner
for the protection of Mourne, and those who,
like him, are working for the sustainable
development of its unique landscape and
cultural heritage.*

*Treat the earth well.
It was not given to you by your parents,
It was loaned to you by your children.*

MASAI PROVERB

Front cover: the wall around High Mourne (see p.104)
Back cover (top to bottom): summit cairn of Lamagan (see
p.40); roofless house and rowan (see p.114); grazing the
hillsides (see p.123)

THE MOUNTAINS OF MOURNE

A Celebration of a Place Apart

DAVID KIRK

Appletree Press

*The Mountains of Mourne have something to teach
or instil, but to learn their lesson or catch their
influence, one must do more than merely glance at
them as though they were a picture book; one must
approach them in a submissive spirit and wait for
what they have to reveal with the passing hours,
and days, and seasons, and years – and having
gazed and gone away one must come back again
and again.*

LOUISE McKAY, 1837

Contents

FOREWORD

BY DAWSON STELFOX

THE MOUNTAINS of Mourne have had an overwhelming influence on my life. To paraphrase Patrick Kavanagh, when their story is told "a carbon copy will unfold my being"[1]

From early family rambles and teenage adventures, by the time I was 16 the Mournes had become my obsession. At every opportunity I was there and in between I was voraciously reading everything I could: Estyn Evans, Praeger, the faded blue rock climbing guide and the instructional bible – Blackshaw's *Mountaineering*. I discovered the delights of camping in high and wild places, the hardships and pleasures of bivouacing in caves, under shelter-stones and in the open, and the overwhelming satisfaction of unravelling the secrets of the cliffs by discovering routes up and through them. By the time I joined Queen's University Mountaineering Club I was already hooked, and the Mournes were my playground. Even though we ventured further and further away – Donegal, Scotland, the Alps, South America, the Himalaya – the Mournes remained and still remain the ever-present source of inspiration, satisfaction and revelation.

Why is this? Is it just parochial prejudice, or do the Mountains of Mourne really have some special combination of qualities that feeds this addiction?

They are not as wild or remote as Donegal. They do not offer the high mountain challenges of Kerry, or the sheer verticality of the cliffs of Fair Head. But even the gentlest of walks in the Mournes gives deep rewards and some of the most difficult climbs in the country can be sought out. Crucially, they offer a perfect balance of accessibility and wildness that creates a very human scale, epitomized by the tight interaction of people and landscape in the foothills gradually giving way to the power of natural forces in the high mountains. It is in that balance – the tenuous relationship between man and nature – that lies the essence of the attraction of a landscape that has shaped its people every bit as much as they have shaped it by quarrying, farming and walking.

The majority of people in Ireland are at most but a few generations away from the land. My mother's family still farms in the foothills and have grazing rights in the high Mournes. My father's parents lived for 20 years in Newcastle and for them the choice was based on the rich botanical resources of the hills. For me and my family the Mournes are fundamentally a playground – an ever more important escape from the pressures of work, back to the simplicity of a small cottage high in the hills, absorbed by the silence, broken only by the bark of a fox or the haunting calls of raven and peregrine.

The traditional cottages of the Mournes are not just compatible with the landscape, they are an integral part of it. Everything about them – position, design, materials, is directly responsive to their surroundings and reflect a deep understanding of the overwhelming forces of nature. They settle into the ground, face away from the prevailing winds and use trees and walls for shelter.

Not so the modern bungalow, thumbing its nose at nature with its double-glazed upvc picture windows, arrogantly set high, exposed against the skylines, selfishly stealing views whilst robbing the rest of us of ours. We have lost the craft, the intuition of building sensitively in the countryside of Ireland – a subtle and sophisticated skill the loss of which we will all soon regret.

There are also, however, threats in over-protection based on regulations and policies – the bureaucracy of state care can lead to the sanitation of the elemental experience; the dead hand of worthiness stifles the adventure. This has been the inevitable reaction to the selfish destruction of the last 30 or 40 years as the conscience of the state tries to react to the threats to what we collectively hold dear. But it is still a fragmented reaction with no single planning or management body, still no national park status with the enhanced protection such designation could bring.

Most important, however, is to forge amongst everyone a deeper understanding of the nature of mountains, of the subtle relationships – and the rewards. *The Mountains of Mourne* is quite a remarkable book in the way it manages to explore and illustrate those relationships. The text and photographs epitomize both the hard reality of mountain life and a mystical romanticism that overwhelms the senses. It demonstrates the centuries-old and changing relationships we have had with the Mournes and makes a powerful argument for re-inventing those relationships for the next generation – based on understanding and care.

When I campaigned to stop the Mourne Wall Walk in the 1980s it was not to stop people's enjoyment or stop them getting out into the hills, but to prevent what had become a physical challenge, undertaken for a badge of achievement, from destroying the very essence of the mountain fabric. Getting the balance right between use and abuse can be achieved by rules, regulations, guidelines and the official paraphernalia of notices, signs and wardens. But wouldn't it be so much better if we did not need to be told how to appreciate and care for the mountains, but understood them within ourselves?

Above all, this is a book of celebration – of the power, beauty, complexity and wonder of the Mountains of Mourne, their meaning and resonances. A celebration of not just the Mournes but of all mountains, a celebration of a natural world that is there for us to enjoy – and care for.

1 Patrick Kavanagh, *Monaghan Hills*

The hills, rock-ribbed and ancient as the sun.

Bryant

On Ben Crom

INTRODUCTION

BORN IN fire, shaped by ice, gentled by rain and sun and living things, the Mountains of Mourne are a place apart, and they occupy a unique place in the brotherhood of mountains and in the hearts of those who have been touched by their spell.

For people around the world in whose veins runs even a drop of Celtic blood the Mountains of Mourne are held in a remarkable affection. For the generations, of all ages and backgrounds, who have rambled and scrambled their paths and rocky slopes, studied their stone, sought their flowers and listened to the music of their streams, they are revered as a very special wilderness haven. For millions who may never have walked them, or even looked on them, but know them through folklore, picture and song, they evoke a singular nostalgia, seeming almost to embody Ireland's mystical heritage.

H V Morton wrote: 'The Mountains of Mourne ... are different from the blue hills of Donegal, different from the weird peaks of Kerry or the wild highlands of the West; yet they are linked to all these by that unearthly quality of the Irish landscape which I can describe only as something half in this world and half in the next.' (*In Search of Ireland*)

Cast in granites that are the island's youngest rock, with spreading skirts of ancient shales patterned by the heat of the deep crucible, the Mournes display an exuberance of scenery that belies their modest area and unassuming stature. With enticing valleys and tracks offering a ready welcome from every side, they are a mountain world of easy familiarity, but for those who seek out their secret places no day there need ever end without some new charm discovered, some new drama observed – as simple as a bright blossom coy in a mossy crevice, as exquisite as the sparkling of crystal or of dancing water, as sublime as earth and elements in conflict. And ever there is, as Robert Lloyd Praeger treasured: 'the solace and joy that comes with quiet wandering on foot along brown streams and among windy hills'. (*The Way That I Went*)

This is a legacy to be cherished. *The Mountains of Mourne* is a celebration of it – a celebration in interweaving photographic and literary images to share with others the things that make it so precious. Hopefully those who know the mountains (including the many who know them much better than I) may see long-familiar facets of them through fresh eyes

and to those who have not yet walked among them, or never will, it will bring a real appreciation of their magic. Most importantly, I hope it will inspire in all a lasting appreciation of the vigilance and care essential if generations to come are to inherit such legacies undiminished.

Caring can take many forms; there is not any interested person who cannot be its agent to some measure. Some have influence – even power – they can exercise to protect, some have skills in stone and wood to repair damage and prevent further, some teach and can guide the young to care, the walker can stoop and lift the bit of litter along his way. There is no time ever to think: 'It's someone else's responsibility'.

Many 'love' the mountains of the earth, but love and care are not the same. The Mournes typify many mountain worlds under pressure; such worlds deserve our care; love alone is not always careful. Ask not . . .

Eternal sentinals, the sculpted pillars of Commedagh look out over the southern lands. Were these the Watchers that gave the mountain its name?

With purple cloak and skirt of forest green, Slieve Donard looks across the sea that bathes its feet.

The mountains lie against one another in soft and gentle lines. They thrust their feet into pine woods and the clouds swing above their heads . . . The green waters of the Irish Sea break almost among the woodlands at the feet of these mountains.

H V MORTON – *IN SEARCH OF IRELAND*

11

THE MAGIC OF MOURNE

AMONG THE swelling pillows of granite that bask in the sun and cause the wind to sigh on the peak called Doan is one small patch of comfortably soft and level grass, just big enough to peg down your tent and stretch out in comfort.

On this spot you are at the very heart of the circular cluster of proud peaks, plunging valleys, armoured buttresses and sparkling cascades that are The Mountains of Mourne.

Doan is not high; a playful jumble, a tumble of rock curving 500 feet up from the heathered plain around it, the 'baby' of the mountains, always seeming to enjoy being the centre of attention of its brothers and sisters around it.

But for the scene that more than any other reveals the wilderness magic of the Mournes none compares with the panorama from its sculpted summit, a great horseshoe of flowing skylines and ice-curved passes, arms outstretched to the south as if to embrace the warming sun.

To the ancient ones, those who settled around the mountain fringes between the steep rocky slopes above and the marshlands below, and who first etched out the tracks that 300 generations later the rambler now treads, spirits dwelled in every watching peak and stone, every chattering stream, every tree and storm cloud. The sounds of the elements were their voices; the capricious moods of mountains their humours.

Around Doan it often seems mountain spirits still work mystery and magic, mixing rock and water, light and life, to weave spells that draw you back and back again, no matter how familiar to you are the mountains and their secret places.

An August evening, camping on Doan after a typical flustery Mournes day of showers and sunlight. As the sun went to its rest behind the western hills the wind died, the valleys filled with a rosy haze which climbed the slopes to the purple-etched skylines. The stillness was absolute, an end to time itself. The dam lights reflected like motionless stars from the water of the sinuous reservoir in the Silent Valley below and bewitched Lough Shannagh turned to burnished mercury.

A cushion of moss wears an early morning diadem of dewdrops.

12

Doan's gentled summit cups a spoonful of sky, watched over by Bearnagh's rugged peaks.

From below the knobbled cliffs two ravens soared up, circling, swooping, looping around each other in a faultless choreography of free spirit. For perhaps 15 minutes their joyful cavort round the summit was the only movement in an ethereal world, the rush of the air through their spread feathers as they swept by the only sound.

Sometimes, as if the mountains have drawn them to be there at the right place at the right time, the Mournes can bless the walker with a once in many lifetimes experience. Seeing, for instance, again from

Doan, that rare and unearthly vision known as a Brocken Spectre, a huge human shape that is your own shadow thrown by a low sun onto a mist bank, mimicking your every movement, and surrounded by a rainbow halo.

For all of his time the moon has been to man the most potent symbol of primeval forces, magical powers, and walking the mountains under its light, the monochromed hills curves of blackness against a star-pierced sky really is, to borrow Morton's words again, like being 'half in this world, half in the next'

The darker magic of other worlds cast a spell over the Mournes on another crystal, August night. Midnight passing, the dark shroud of a total eclipse was thrown over a full moon that had shone high over Slieve Binnian and reflected off the waters below with silvery brilliance, and the mountains and valleys became a baleful, alien world filled with blood-red menace.

Moments of such outstanding beauty and drama are incomparable experiences, privileges (that make up for all the 'bad' days of rain and pain!) but the affection, the veneration, in which the Mountains of Mourne have been held by successive generations is the measure of the wealth and diversity of their simpler charms.

How many young people, under the spell of the Mournes from a first magical night under the stars, lulled by a stream's murmuring, have been inspired to pursue lifetimes of challenge and fulfilment, brilliant days of adventure and freedom – and a store of mountain memories for later years when high summits must be gazed upon from far below? For how many have early scrambles up their heathered slopes led on to Earth's highest and wildest places?

The Mountains of Mourne have known the touch and sounds of human life since nomad families first crossed the widening sea to hunt and fish an island teeming once again with life after the long dead ice years. They served the generations well, providing them with food and water, stone and refuge, grazing

The Mountains of Mourne as seen from the heights above Carlingford. A long inlet of the sea, once ice-filled, separates the Mournes from their sisters to the south, the knobbly Carlingford Mountains. Although of the same age they differ in their geological history and rock types.

The Mountains of Mourne seem to float like a distant citadel above the farmlands of County Down.

for their stock and fuel for their fires. But it was 10,000 years (years which changed the face of their landscape) before they came to be cherished for more – for themselves, their challenge and charm; a place to walk with nature, a place for relaxation rather than toil, a place to rest mind and test body, to get away.

It was less than 200 years ago that the new breed of nineteenth-century naturalists and travel-writers began to arouse society (or at least the portion of it that had the means and the leisure to respond) to an appreciation of wilderness areas, their fascination and their magic, but they were still perceived by most as an alien environment, no place for the genteel (a gentility, of course, sans vibram, sans Goretex, sans map, compass or energy bar). The surveyor John O'Donovan reflected his time when, in 1834, he viewed the Mournes from Slieve Donard and reported them to be 'a wild and dismal region of the barrenest mountains . . . lonely and desolate, and will remain so to the end of time'.

But sixty years later Praeger was writing with the infectious enthusiasm that would inspire generations of fellow naturalists and ramblers: 'There is a marvellous charm about these great brown hills, where the silence is broken only by the murmuring of the streams and the bleatings of the sheep; these huge walls of granite, tenanted by the peregrine and the raven; these deep quiet valleys and these lonely mountain tarns.'

Mountains and minds were opening to each other and the seeds were being sown of a love affair that grows stronger with every decade. Today, another century on, the hills of 'good grey rock that loves the grasping hand' (see 'Epilogue', p.135) are rarely lonely.

A Very Singular Place

PUTTING A good foot before you the longest one-way walk through the Mountains of Mourne, between the resort towns of Newcastle in the north-east and Rostrevor in the south-west, can be done in a day; a fair stretch of the legs. Half a day by track and pass, and a feast of scenery, will get you from one side to the other, and with time left for a beer, maybe two.

Just fifteen miles by seven or so, as the ravens fly, the Mournes are singular in the sheer variety of mountain experience packed into a space so compact. In spite of their small area and deceptively gentle outline, these are real mountains, with more than their share of drama and challenge, an atmospheric world of muscle-cramping slopes and rocky crags, steep ravines and high moorland, reflective loughs, companionable streams and space washed through with ever-changing light. These mountains bear noble names given by ancient peoples, names that resonate with the folk memories of many millennia – Commedagh, Lamagan, Binnian, Bearnagh, Shannagh . . .

But wilderness does not mean remoteness; it is the accessibility of an area offering so much that makes it so special. Twisting, dipping roads hem the skirts of the mountain; others cross them by pass and valley first used by great glaciers shouldering their way south, dividing the range into three areas, of decreasing stature and diverse nature, known to those who live around them as the High, the Middle and the Western Mournes. Even the least accessible areas of mountain challenge can be reached with little more than an hour's walk-in.

The high pass that separates the headwaters of the Shimna and the White Water rivers, one cascading northwards from the mountains the other draining southern slopes, forms the narrow waist of the range, and it carries the ancient roadway that since the time of the first settlers has been an important route between the farmlands of the inland 'back side' of the Mournes and Kilkeel, fishing-port and market town of the rich and secluded plain bounded by mountain and sea, the Kingdom of Mourne.

East of this divide cluster the proud High Mournes, to many THE Mountains of Mourne although their area is less than half that of the whole range. The dramatic, scenic and romantic mountains beloved of painter and poet, rambler and climber, they are a tight family of twelve distinguished granite peaks, presided over by their patriarch, Slieve Donard, a

A winter sun comes to melt the frost that coats the stones of Binnian.

majestic mountain presence in spite of rising to less than 3,000 feet.

At the coast these forest-fringed High Mournes bathe their feet in the cold green water of the Irish Sea, leaving barely enough room for the first miles of the stone-dyked, fuchsia-fringed road that is the northern gateway to the Kingdom of Mourne. Their northern boundary is the valley of the lovely Shimna River which curves round to join the sea at Newcastle, flowing by deep mysterious pools, cool mossy boulders and sparkling cascades under the venerable trees of Tollymore Forest.

The Middle Mournes lie in a triangle between the Kilkeel Road and the Alpine-like Kilbroney Valley, a deep, fault-formed trough, shaped and smoothed by a thousand feet of moving ice and the melt-water torrents that followed. Spreading from their apex at Slievenaman, the mountains rise steadily as far as their mid-point before gradually descending again as the granite gives way to slate which plunges steeply into the deep sea waters of Carlingford Lough.

Mostly the middle range contains gentler and softer mountains than their macho brethren to the East, more grass than heather, easier on leg (if often wetter on feet) but with charm and interest in full measure and a delicacy of their own. If the high mountains are the lads of Mourne, these are the lasses. The exception is their tallest member, iron-clad Eagle Mountain with its glowering, gullied eastern bastion, the highest cliff face in all of Mourne, seeming almost to have strayed into the wrong place.

West of the Kilbroney Valley and the road it carries to Rostrevor, lie a third series of Mourne ridges.

Mountains are the beginning and end of all natural scenery.

JOHN RUSKIN

The Mournes from the dunes of Murlough Nature Reserve.

Only about 25 square miles in area and laced with narrow lanes and streams they are foothills to the mountains. With softer weather and kinder soil their plant and animal life is richer and several are cultivated over their summits. As the granites of Mourne slip gently out of sight again beneath the ancient shales from which they thrust so dramatically to the east, the hills gradually merge into the rich drumlin landscape. But by lane or by wall there is still pleasant walking to be enjoyed here; indeed, for a colourful high summer tramp the undulating ridge of Slieve Roosley has no equal in all the mountains for its spreading blaze of purple heather.

Walter Harris – 'The Antient and Present State of the County of Down' 1744

A deep and narrow vale divides Slieve Donard from Slieve Snavan or the Creeping Mountain, so called because it must be climbed in a creeping posture* – and through this vale winds a pretty serpentine stream which discharges itself into the sea on the eastward of the mountains. The Creeping Mountain stands to the SW of this stream and presents to the view a huge rock, resembling at a distance an old fortification, very high, overhanging and detached, as it were, from the eastern side of this mountain. After rain a stream rushes from the west side of the said rock which, shooting from the top, falls in a large cascade to the east of which is a huge natural cave, affording an entrance as wide as the cave itself. This frightful chamber is lined with fern grass and several other mountain plants, and inhabited by a vast number of hawks, jackdaws, owls etc. and at the further ends of it the light breaks through natural crevices. To the left of this cave you climb up through a very

Cave on lower Cove Mountain

narrow passage to the top of the rock and land on one of the most beautiful, most magnificent and romantic spots that can well be conceived. One there finds that the rock mentioned is only the advanced part of a large shelf which projects at about half the height of the mountain with a sweep and leaves the space of about two acres on the top. Round the north-west, the west and the south of this area the mountain rises to a great height and stand like vast wall. The area itself is almost round and slopes gently from all sides towards the middle, where is formed a beautiful lake, circular also and clear as crystal. As the soil of this spot seems tolerably good, if nature were a little helped and it were cut into circular terraces and slopes and embellished with flowers it would make perhaps one of the most grand and beautiful improvements in the world.

*The 'vale' is the Annalong Valley and Snavan is Lamagan and Cove mountains, then regarded as one

Now a lonely, shrinking pool on the Cove Mountain shelf, 250 years ago this was 'a beautiful lake, circular and clear as crystal'.

The Annalong Valley

. . . on the highest peak of a wild and dismal region of the barrenest mountains, exposed to every storm, far removed from every land producing food for the sustenance of man. For to this day there is not a human being to be seen throughout the mountains or valleys for a considerable extent in any direction! The region is dismal; lonely and desolate and will remain so to the end of time, its rocky and rugged steep surfaces defying the hand of cultivation.

JOHN O'DONOVAN – *ORDNANCE SURVEY LETTER*, APRIL 1834

Sitting on a high, naked peak, surveying an immense region, I can say to myself: here you are on ground which stretches to the bowels of the earth – no more recent layer, no piles of ruins, have come between you and the primeval world; you do not walk over a continuous grave as in those fertile valleys. These peaks have produced nothing living and have devoured nothing living; they are before all life and above all life.

JOHANN WOLFGANG VON GOETHE – 'ABOUT GRANITE', 1784

The lesser fragments from the granite rotted many millennia ago have long since been washed and blown away, leaving these stones to crown Binnian's north tor like abandoned building blocks.

In the Beginning

FOR MAYBE 30 million long years the granites had waited in darkness for the elements to weather away, grain by grain, the mile of rock under which they were imprisoned. On the surface above and across the earth new orders of life were evolving.

Then, at one moment in unmeasured time, as a final fragment of their cover was washed or blown or scraped away, light pierced down into the rock through the first clear quartz to glint in the sun; at some spot in the ancient landscape the patient granites emerged at last into the realm of light and life, ahead of them the many long millennia that it would take to shape them into the Mountains of Mourne.

The granite which today grips the walker's boot, and shapes the scenery that uplifts his spirit, took form in the era of cataclysm that began 65 million years ago and which lasted for a quarter of that time. Continents sundered and new oceans spread and rock was stretched and ruptured. Thin liquid basalt from deep in the earth poured out through the fractures, building thick layers which buried the northern chalklands of Ireland. Time after time new landscapes were created, cooling, bearing life which flourished in tropical luxury until it was destroyed by the next flood of magma boiling across them.

To the south east fiery volcanoes built high and darkened the skies. Today the hills of Carlingford and Slieve Gullion mark their passing. Nearby, but more than a mile down in the tormented earth, vast caverns opened up as ancient shales fractured. Great blocks split off to sink slowly into a thick and viscous magma. This magma, distilled from remelted sediments from the earth's oldest continents, long since returned to the fires below, surged round and over the sinking blocks to fill the widening voids. Six times over five million years this happened, with each new up-pouring of magma slowly chilling and crystallising into casts of granite, ready for the distant time when the elements would free and fashion them.

Once bubbles in the hardening granite magma in which sparkling crystals grew, these exposed and weathered 'drusy' cavities on Chimney Rock Mountain now sparkle with clear rainwater that collects in them.

21

'Rock'

Sing of the rock once molten,
Now in silence.
Grass grows not, nor tree
But rock
    Lives . . .

    Slowly . . .
Slowly the granite mass
Thinks down the year-avenues
Knowing
    slowly
      the centuries
Seeing the years as seconds –
        sands –

    Their poetry
    The poetry
Of slow fire kindling,
Of rocks red-hot
    and white-flaming
Their music of slow beginnings
    And slow lives,
Long crystal symphonies –
Alive for a million years –
Consciousness stretched back
    like a road.

Sing of the rocks
Cooling to consciousness
    Fire in their veins
      And flame in their beginnings.
Sing of the slow rocks.

Keith Battarbee

The high cliffs of Spellack

Ben Crom's sculpted tors frame the north summit of Binnian
on the opposite side of the Silent Valley.

Erosion in action – the elements gouge gullies and carve rock sculptures on Slieve Commedagh.

Mountains, you are growing old;
Your ribs of granite are getting weak and rotten.

E M Morse

Sheep graze the grassy banks of Shanky's River near Leitrim Lodge.

So long as the land has mountains,
Forests and pastures,
So long will the earth survive.

HINDU TEXT

THE SHAPING

A SABRE-TOOTH tiger, or one of man's earliest primate ancestors, could have set the first living foot on the granite of Mourne when it appeared on the surface of a sub-tropical Irish landscape. Acacia, cinnamon and palm rooted in its soils. Granite would have rotted away quickly in the warm, moist conditions but those days were almost at the end of Ireland's time in such a climate. Global temperatures were falling, Europe continued its long drift north, carrying Ireland into cooler latitudes, with physical erosion, to which granite is more resistant, gradually superseding the aggressive chemical weathering.

During these aeons the softer, sedimentary rocks of Co Down which entombed the granites were raised many times above the neighbouring landscapes by the heavings of a still restless earth; raised up only to be worn down to sea level with even greater vigour. The granites appeared first just as gentle swellings on the level plains. They increased in number as the surface around them was lowered, and grew to become hills and eventually mountains, proud, tall. As they rose the same elements that were freeing them from their slaty prison worked to shape them also. They sought out the weak spots of the hard rock, as they still do, dissolving it, chipping at it here, abrading it there. Over the countless years they rounded the sharp edges of the massive blocks and planed flat platforms around the emerging peaks; they turned the fractures of their ancient cooling into gullies and valleys and washed their crystal fragments down them to the seas.

The rocky summits, split and rent,

Formed turret, dome or battlement,

Or seemed fantastically set

With cupola or minaret

SIR WALTER SCOTT

Binnian tor

Donard gazes benignly down as two swans pass on their way to
the rich coastal feeding grounds below his northern flanks.

*Slieve Donard does not torture you on the last mile
as Goatfell does in the Isle of Arran or as Ben
Nevis does after you leave the half-way hut; he is a
decent, kindly mountain with no evil in him but
sufficient hardness to make you respect him, and
yourself, when at last you fling yourself down by
the cairn on top.*

H V MORTON – *IN SEARCH OF IRELAND*

Puffs of summer cloud drift lazily past Slieve Binnian

Slievenaglogh

The ramparts of a godhead's dwelling.

THOMAS MOORE

'By Gulley'

It was an idea conceived in the autumn of 1982 – a traverse of the Mournes using some of the major gullies.

Some early morning organisation enabled us to set out from Donard Park at 7 am, having earlier deposited our getaway car at Attical. The date, August 13, in no way deterred us.

An early morning view of the Mourne peaks, thrusting up from a valley of white mist had left us impatient to get into the hills. The weather was in no way reminiscent of any day we had been in the Mournes before. It was hot, and bound to become hotter, so that by the time we reached our first gulley at the Pot of Pulgarve on Commedagh all excess clothing had been discarded and the little that was left was soaked in sweat.

The first gulley we took at our leisure, a sort of a warm-up.

We descended to the Pot of Legawherry, where we fairly buzzed up a longish gulley to the left hand side of the pot. Buzz was the operative word as some third of the way up we discovered the rocks were swarming with bees. Had they attacked we would have added a new dimension to the word 'scrambling'.

We proceeded in good heart across Slieve Beg, this time reversing our earlier ploy by descending the gully to the right of the Devil's Coachroad, with Satan Buttress on our left. Normally this gulley drips water but we had dry granite sand which flowed down it.

The next gulley was Skye-Pye on Cove and traversing across we climbed into it. The tempo was slowly increasing. This was a satisfying scramble, long and demanding. On the top of Cove we discussed the best route to Summit Gulley on Ben Crom.

The scrambling on Ben Crom is magnificent and the blaeberries were the biggest, the best and the most plentiful we had yet encountered. They were to provide us with an unexpected source of sustenance during the day. Summit Gulley was to be the most exciting and demanding yet it will be remembered for an unusual visitor. A homing pigeon flew in and perched beside us. Maybe like ourselves it was getting tired or perhaps it was looking for protection from the kestrel that had earlier been scouting the area.

Great Gulley on Eagle Mountain was next on the schedule but it seemed a long walk away and we wanted something in between. The cliffs of Slieve Muck, close to Carn, beckoned. Here is an interesting gulley with a needle's eye and we were lucky it was snuff dry but judging by the moss on the rock it must be nasty when wet. The chimney and the needle's eye are too narrow to take a man and a rucksack so we had to haul the sacks up by rope.

Pigeon Rock Mountain was the penultimate hurdle, but it seemed somehow to have grown as we wearily picked our way over it. The chat and the banter had been good all day but now it died away. However, once again the knowledge of water ahead added a spring to our step and we must have drunk gallons.

It was to be the last watering hole, the little stream that flows from Windy Gap, and we knew it. We finished practically the last of our food and it took real effort to forsake the pleasure of lying beside running water and continue towards our final goal. This was to be the climax of the day; the icing on the cake, so to speak, the climb up Great Gulley. As we climbed higher into the bowels of what even on a fine day was an awesome place, we all had, I am sure, the same thought – 'How am I going to climb that bloody step?' To Victor was given the honour. He

The great gulley of Ben Crom is lit by the dawn light reflecting from the reservoir below.

was conned into sussing it out. While he was engaged in this delicate operation, a series of indelicate sounds were heard which suggested that far from having the wind up some members were experiencing wind-out. Maybe it is the same thing. After a bit of scrabbling, heaving and pushing we were up 'the step'. The rock formation at the top of the gully leered down on the five who had scrambled on their feet, so confident now they couldn't wait to get to the top. Here the feeling was good. A tremendous spirit of well-being embraced the group and the tiredness was replaced by something which made the walk-out a pleasure. The smell of bog myrtle on a soft Mourne evening will be a reminder of Great Gulley and a great day.

The big walks are there in abundance in these islands, big enough to write a book about, big enough to write two books, but make no mistake, the Mournes can live in any company when it comes to providing a memorable day.

FREDDIE MCCANN – 'BY GULLEY' FROM PEAK VIEWING – THE JOURNAL OF THE NI MOUNTAIN LEADER TRAINING BOARD, 1983

'On the Plateau'

Crisp, wind-moulded snow on Donard sparkles in early sunlight.

This is your hour in time: remember it.
It will not come again. Rehearse it well
And cherish it against the day to come
When you may go no more upon the hills.

Here is the sullen mystery of rock,
The heart-break stubborn stillness of the
    hills,
The diamond-dazzle treachery of snow.

Here dwells the death-wish, under the
smooth snow,
. . . only to lie down
Lie down for ever in the sheet-white snow,
For ever, to lie down alone . . .

This is your hour in time, in which you
    know
That it is possible to be yourself and free
From sweetly overwhelming tides of love
For friends who walk the valleys there
    below . . .

This is your virgin hour, crystallise
And keep for ever safe from seeking hands.

EILIDH NISBET

Winter sunrise at Binnian Lough

The deep and thoughtful quiet of winter

J R R TOLKIEN – *THE LORD OF THE RINGS*

Wind-sculpted snow

Ice - The Master Sculptor

THE LONG shaping of the Mountains of Mourne to their present outlines was virtually complete when a million and a half arctic years chilled the once warm granite to its heart, splintering the rock faces and driving life from the valleys and slopes. Temperatures fluctuated dramatically, with brief warm phases that allowed life to re-establish a hold only to be banished again by the another long, deep, freeze. Through other millennia, when the atmosphere turned more moist, endless snows built thick ice-sheets that spread, remorselessly grinding, across the land; the master-sculptor came to carve the final touches to the mountain landscape

The moving ice, sometimes from the north and sometimes the west, at times higher than most of the mountains themselves, scraping round their flanks, squeezing between them, jousted with the glaciers spilling from the high corries for possession of the valleys. Their skirmishes left behind a mountain world of elegant curves, aloof rock buttresses with spreading skirts of splintered debris, boulders perched high above their birthplace and valleys layered with the pulverised rocks of the surfaces over which the ice had ground its way. These swathes and mounds of sands, gravels and boulders in chaotic mix, were left to coat the mountain hollows as, 15,000 years ago, the last ice sheets lifted their siege and melted away, defeated by a returning warmth that still prevails.

The ice returned to the oceans; life returned to the mountains.

The High Mournes wear a winter coat.

The Pot of Legawherry, one of the most picturesque in Mourne, at the head of the Spinkwee River, is a deep depression surrounded on three sides by cliffs and pinnacles of granite. Shanslieve, Slieve Commedagh and Slieve Corragh all plunge down a thousand feet into the lonely grassy hollow where the never-ending rustling of the streamlets alone breaks the silence.

ROBERT LLOYD PRAEGER – *OFFICIAL GUIDE TO COUNTY DOWN, 1900*

Sunlight spills out of the great Pot of Legawherry – once a deep glacier spilled out of the most dramatic corrie in the Mournes.

35

Bearnagh's snowy cape catches the morning light.

'Great Mountains Love Great Storms'

Great mountains love great storms,
and lesser hills long rain.
They reach their arms in riotous ridge forms
to hail cloud-comrades from the drenching
plain:
their gorges drain the upward rush of thunder;
their torrents, speeding under,
pour back the lees to breed cloud-riot again.

Great mountains hold harsh truth,
and lesser heights long trust.
The warring crests make comrades of our youth,
burnish our manhood, rasp our spirit-rust:
kind hills bend for our age a gentler shoulder,
staying our hearts, grown older,
with hope new-fashioned from our faltering
dust.

GEOFFREY WINTHROP YOUNG

Praeger in Mourne

The name of Slieve Bignion recalls the day when I saw, and felt, weather at its very worst; and it is not often that one does that, even as regards summer weather. The occasion was an excursion of the Belfast Naturalists Field Club and the programme was to drive to the entrance of the Happy Valley (now the Silent Valley), climb Slieve Bignion and walk through the mountains to Newcastle – a tough menu for a mixed party. In those hardy days it was a rule that excursions started regardless of the weather, and were carried through unless that proved impracticable. We reached Happy Valley to encounter a south-easterly gale howling in from the Irish Sea, and a sky that meant mischief. Half of the party decided to stay with the wagonettes (no buses in those days) and the other half started up the valley. The weather worsened rapidly; heavy rain began. When we got to the point where we should turn to the right up the steep slope of Slieve Bignion there were only three of us left, and half-way up two more gave out. The Secretary (myself), left alone, decided to maintain the Club tradition and put the programme through. There was comparative shelter till the vicinity of the crowning crags was reached; then the furious gusts compelled me to hands and knees, and even so I was twice rolled over. I wormed my way in to the topmost crags, among which the gale shrieked and yelled; one would have been afraid to venture had not everything around been solid granite. As it was the rocks seemed to sway and cower under the furious buffets. I could not show my face for every drop of rain stung as if it had been a flying pebble; it was an exhilarating and almost terrifying struggle, and an interesting lesson in what exposure really means. When I dropped back behind the crest my raincoat was in ribbons and my hat was gone; I was drenched and battered and sorely out of breath – but I had done it! Then of course came the reward of virtue. The wind dropped as quickly as it had risen, the clouds broke, and three hours later I swung into Newcastle in bright sunshine, ahead of time. Those were the days!

ROBERT LLOYD PRAEGER – THE WAY THAT I WENT

Spindrift blowing across Bearnagh's slopes.

For the man sound in body and serene of mind there is no such thing as bad weather; every sky has its beauty and storms which whip the blood do but make it pulse more vigorously.

GEORGE GISSING

Hen Mountain

Misty day on Donard

Mountains on whose barren breast
The labouring clouds do often rest.

JOHN MILTON

38

*A sedentary life is the real sin against the Holy
Spirit. Only those thoughts that come by walking
have any value.*

FREIDRICH NIETZSCHE

'Ireland'

O, these lakes and all gills that live in them,
These acres and all the legs that walk on them,
The tall winds and all wings that cling to them,
Are part and parcel of me, bit and bundle,
Thumb and thimble. Them I am, but none more
Than the Mountains of Mourne that turn and
    trundle
Roundly like slow coils of oil along the shore
Of Down and on inland. When I begin
To draw my memory's nets and outlines in,
Then through its measured mesh escapes the fuss
And fluster of all finicky things.
Of the Mournes I remember most the mist,
The grey granite goosefleshed, the minute
And blazing parachutes of fuchsia, and us,

The summit cairn of Lamagan framed
by Donard's cloud-tipped cone.

Listening to the tiny clustered clinks
Of little chisels tinkling tirelessly
On stone, like the drip of birds' beaks picking
Rapidly at scattered grain. I think of those
Wet sodden days when we, for miles and miles,
Steadily padded the slow sponge of turf
That squealed and squelched between our bared
    toes;
Or on airy ridge, urgent and agile, ran,
A chain of jiggling figures on the skyline;
Or, skilfully in file, followed, tricking
The hoops of hairy bramble in our path,
Poking in undergrowth and picking
The bitter berries that prickle the springs
Of the dark mouth. There was Bloody River
Where the granite pickles bristled and blazed, and
Ebullient water bellied over
Boulders with the sweep of bell's shoulders,
And pancaked out in pools. Drinnahilly
Where the gales smoothed and glued back the
    eyelids;
The granite river that is called Kilkeel,
Whose beds were clean and gritty like oatmeal;
And Commedagh in whose high summer heat
Nothing stirred, only the shimmering bleat
Of sheep; and we, as we sat and chattered,
Marked the motionless shine of falls far off
On Bignion, and nothing else mattered;
And Legawherry so soft and grassy,
Where the white scuts lazily scattered,
And never in their remotest burrows,
Did ferret-fear come closely after them;
Slieve-na-brock and its long pig-tail trickles
That hung down the bald rocks, reaching to

Summertime adventure at Bloody Bridge

The glossy backs of the bracken. And Donard
Where, high over all hanging, the strong hawk
Held in his eyes whole kingdoms, sources, seas,
And in his foot-hooks felt all things wriggling
Like the single string of river niggling
Among the enormous mountain bottoms.
Bearnagh and Lamagan and Chimney Rock,
Spelga, Pulgarve, and Cove – all these names lie
Silently in my grass grown memory,

Each one bright and steady as a frog's eye;
But touch it and it leaps, leaps like a bead
Of mercury that breaks and scatter
Suddenly in a thousand shining strings
And running spools and ever-dwindling rings
Round the mind's bowl, till at last all drop,
Lumped and leaden again, to one full stop.

W R RODGERS

Glowing against a reflected sky, a clump of harestail cotton grass has its own private island in a calm pool among the peat hags.

The infinite has written its name on the heavens in shining stars and on the earth in tender flowers.

JEAN PAUL RICHTER

Here are cool mosses deep,
And through the moss the ivies creep.

ALFRED, LORD TENNYSON

A mushroom snuggles up to the shelter of a granite boulder.

VEGETATION
The plants return

ALGAE AND lichen were the first to make it back into the mountains. Mosses splashed gold, red and vivid green and built peat even on the thick layers of permafrost ice that long remained in deep hollows. Hairy grey rhacomitrium moss climbed high; it still survives by sheltering between the sharp shards of rock on the highest peaks. The sedges and rushes and grasses followed, finding nourishment in the glacial soils but in turn mixing their remains with the granite grits to build new soils higher and higher up the mountain sides. Seeds blown from the far south or carried by migrating birds could root here bringing the first flowering plants. Small shrubs came, heathers and crowberries, and finally trees, first hardy dwarf juniper; still surviving on arid sites where others cannot live, then tiny wind-resistant willows and birches, hazel and later rowan.

They clothed the Mourne valleys with their first scrubby woodland, edging the shallow lakes that occupied many of them and which, filled in by generations of plant remains, became the first peat bogs. As the weather warmed hazel spread enthusiastically but was soon put in the shade by the woods of oak, ash, and elm spreading across the glacial drift on the lower valley slopes. Alder and willow took the damp places and Scots pine the drier.

The mountains and the plants and the wildlife that teemed among them, lemmings and fox, deer and hare, enjoyed these halcyon conditions for almost four millennia but by 5,000 years ago the climate had begun to slip once again back to wetter ways, the mountain soils becoming leached and the surface waterlogged. Alder flourished but spreading bogland rose around the trunks of the pines and oaks. By 3,000 years ago they had virtually disappeared from the mountain valleys, on the steeper, better drained slopes they escaped the peat but became increasingly stunted as the climate deteriorated.

The changing mixtures of ancient tree pollen that drifted and fell each spring onto that same peat as it grew over the centuries are still preserved there. They show that by then other hands were increasingly at work in changing the mountain scenery for ever, cutting away the remaining tree cover for fuel, for dwellings and for land, speeding the demise of the woodland and the spread of the blanketing bog – the hands of the first farmers.

Probably the highest and hardiest tree in Mourne – This rowan flying like a flag from a rock face on Slieve Bearnagh appears precarious but has survived many years of the frequent fearsome winds that funnel through deep Crom valley.

The changing vegetation

MEASURED BY the lives of man the rock is eternal. St Patrick ministering below, the Iron Age rath-builders, the Bronze-age tomb-builders before them and their ancient forebears gathering shellfish off Murlough sands and berries on the shrubby slopes, watched the sun and the mists play around the same shapes of peak, valley and buttress that are familiar today. They drank from the same dancing streams and the hands of the hunters grasped the same rock ledges that hold the scramblers of the 21st century.

The fortunes of various species of plant life waxed and waned in response to changes of climate throughout the centuries, but the clothing of the slopes today would have seemed a threadbare garb to all of these early people.

Today it is almost as hard to imagine the mountains as once they were, clothed almost to the highest summits with shrubby woodland, as to imagine them as the lifeless, splintered desolation that was left by the ice.

New trees, different trees, now give the foothills an evergreen skirt; above them the rock, and the blanket bog which began its spread six thousand years ago, wears a different, closer mantle, a heathland that, where it has not suffered too much from chomping teeth, sharp hoof and tramping boot, is one of the best developed in Europe.

Summer in the Silent Valley. The vegetation along the lake's western shore, where sheep have been excluded, in the forefront, is luxurious compared with the other hillslopes around.

The boglands below Ben Crom, with Binnian mistily behind. This patch of ground, the ancient lake bed lying between Bearnagh, Meelbeg and Crom is what Robert Praeger described as 'the worst bit of ground in all Mourne'. Its gullied surface is certainly designed to put the walker into an exasperated lather but no place in the mountains is more mystically atmospheric, whether the day be bright or gloomy, than this.

Preserved by the rising peat that drowned it, the roots of a pine lie bleached on a surface once again exposed to the air by the peat-cutting of past farmers tending their cattle on the high summer pastures.

Over much of the Mournes the blanket bog is in recession as frost, wind and rain erode peat exposed by grazing and tramping feet and the collapse of sub-surface drainage channels. In isolated areas, however, peat layers still grow under their lush green caps of sphagnum moss.

Seemingly solid peat is honeycombed by a labyrinth of 'tunnels' which drain away its burden of rainwater into the mountain streams, as this one on Pigeon Rock Mountain.

Erosion has turned Doan's lower slopes into a surreal moonscape.

An isolated hag shows the depth of peat that has been eroded away.

Nature is left to heal the surface of the Black Bog. Pollen grains preserved in these peat layers tell the story of the changing vegetation since the Ice Age.

The marsh is bleak and lonely,
Scarce a flower
Gleams in the waving grass.

CONSTANCE MERRITT

The tiny pool that was Shan Lough, by Pierce's Bog

'Cartin' Peat'

Heavily loaded
From Pierce's Bogs,
Wi' a cart o' peat
The oul' mare jogs.
Slitherin', slidin',
Diggin' in her toes,
Down the Turf Loaney,
The oul' mare goes.

The side o' the mountain
Is desprit steep;
In the summer drought
The dust drifts deep;
Trampled an' tossed
It fills the air;
A thirsty job
For me an' the mare.

Over Altataggart
The hot sun shines
On bright green larch
An' gloomy pines;
But the mountain tops
In the fadin' day
Are muffled and misty
An' far away.

Down the loaney
We lug our load,
O'er the humpbacked bridge
To the Hilltown road.
The long day ends,
And the strong man tires,
But the cart is filled
Wi' our winter fires.

RICHARD ROWLEY

The turf track from Pierce's Bog

Bluebells like blue smoke drifting between the trees in Tollymore.

Among the trees of Tollymore

THE NOW bare hills of Mourne rise almost protectively behind the trees of Tollymore Park crowding round the deep pools and falls of the Shimna River. Extolled as a place of unique charm by visitors for more than 300 years Tollymore was opened for all to enjoy in 1955 when it became Northern Ireland's first forest park, and it remains one of the best-loved of its attractions. The setting of Tollymore, between mountains and sea, the diversity of aspect and the variety of its woodland, dark deep conifer forest, the stately exotics of its arboretum, means there is beauty to be found there at any season of the year, from the smoke-like clouds of bluebells drifting under the fresh green of the first leaves of spring, to the golden months of autumn and the silent stillness of snow-laden boughs in winter.

Strategically located in Tollymore Park is the Northern Ireland Centre for Outdoor Activities, where young (and not so young) people can learn the skills that will allow them to enjoy adventure sports in the mountains and on water with confidence. With the challenges of the outdoors increasingly on the curriculum of schools and youth organisations a vital part of the Centre's work is developing mountain leadership and management skills in those responsible for their safety.

Northern Ireland Centre for Outdoor Activities – Tollymore Mountain Centre

In the deep of
Tollymore Forest

The last dead remnants
of the once widespread
plantations of Kinnahalla
stand like aliens on
points duty.

Tollymore Park

*And when bright
sunset fills
The silver wood
with light*

HENRY WADSWORTH
LONGFELLOW

*Tollymore Park is still a lovely spot, although the
wholesale cutting of fine timber has greatly shorn it
of the beauty which it possessed a quarter of a
century ago . . . it awakens in those who remember
it twenty-five years ago a feeling of sadness when
they consider to what extent the glory is departed.*

WRITTEN IN JUNE 1898 (FOR THE ITINERARY OF AN
EXCURSION TO THE REGION BY MEMBERS OF THE
INCORPORATED GAS INSTITUTE)

– Sentiments that will strike a sympathetic chord with lovers
of Tollymore a hundred years on!

The flowering

ONLY HALF a dozen specimens are now to be found in the Mountains of Mourne of a hardy little species that led the return of flowering plants in the inhospitable but slowly warming bleakness left by the departing ice.

Sheep and competitors more favoured by today's climate have reduced the yellow-flowered Roseroot to just a handful of survivors, the last of the ancient race, clinging to a difficult life on a small stretch of rock face, rooting into deep damp crevices.

The roseroot is a botanical treasure of the Mournes, and there are others waiting to be discovered by anyone who adds interest and fun to their mountain spring and summer days by seeking them out. Although more than half the of the total number of species of flora present in Ireland can be found around the Mournes and their foothills – some 320 species are listed – their uplands cannot display the

Roseroot – last of an ancient race

diversity of flowering plants, especially the alpines, to be found around other ranges. And some that have made a home there are so reclusive that years of exploring the valleys and slopes might not reveal them. But the weight of a good plant guide in the haversack can pay a rich dividend in surprises and discoveries, making it worth the effort; a rare Irish ladies tresses perhaps, or a stag's horn clubmoss.

Meanwhile enjoy the company of the more populous blooms that sprinkle the hills around your feet – bright laughing tormentil, milkwort and hungry butterwort, eyebright, lousewort, the first to awaken to spring, shy violet, the carpeting bedstraw, bog asphodel brightening the sedge beds, perfumed thyme. There are orchids, maybe appearing once in a decade, the rare Marsh St John's wort where water swirls gently, the starry saxifrage, sparkling above emerald moss. . .

Bog Cotton

On the grassy lower Mourne slopes more tender plants such as the harebell find sheltered accommodation among the scattered heather clumps. To the ancients the harebell was the 'elve's thimble' so it maybe also enjoys the protection of other, more elemental, powers.

Full many a flower is born to blush unseen.

THOMAS GRAY

And when the flowers aren't in bloom there are the hundreds of varieties of more modest plants, ground-hugging shrubs, ferns, mosses and clubmosses, sedges, fungi and lichen that paint the rocks – each by its presence describing the habitat which supports it. Ground not affected by draining, burning, grazing or trampling can carry 12 or more species on a square metre.

The gentle and bright flowers soften, counterpoint, the hard world of granite. With nature's immaculate timing, the first of these new forms of plant life were just starting out on their evolutionary journey at the very time the stone of Mourne was cooling to crystal deep below the surface.

Stag's horn clubmoss

Earth laughs in flowers

RALPH WALDO EMERSON

Hawkweed

Starry Saxifrage

Marsh St John's Wort

Bogbean

Bog Asphodel

Wild Thyme

Golden Rod

Eyebright

Heath Bedstraw

Lousewort

To create a little flower is the labour of ages.

WILLIAM BLAKE

Wood sorrel

Tormentil and Milkwort

Heath Spotted Orchid

Speedwell

Carnivorous Sundew

Wood sage

Carnivorous Butterwort

Buttercup

Violet

The purple cloak

SPRING IS tardy and high summer does not linger long in the Mournes which makes it even more exciting when the bright green of the year's new life spreads up the slopes of Robert Lloyd Praeger's 'great brown hills' and a few weeks later they don the purple cloak of heather around their shoulders. Three heathers clothe the Mountain slopes – erica tetralix, the cross-leaved heath, the first to bloom in early summer, with its cap of large, pale-pink flowers on long stems and its preference for the wetter patches of peat, erica cinerea, the bell heather, clothing the middle slopes with rippling swathes of deep purple in mid-summer (the sharp eye will occasionally see rare white-flowered specimens), and the gentle, frothy calluna vulgaris, the ling, with its tiny and lovely pink blossoms, the latest to bloom, the highest growing – and the world record holder for pollen production, with up to 16 billion grains per square metre! While the cross-leaved heath is usually scattered as individual plants, the others spread in great sheets over the hillsides, sometimes of one species alone, at others both intermingled, covering the peat and scrambling through the boulder fields, rooting everywhere from seeping bog to cracks in arid rock faces.

A purple cushion of erica cinerea shows that life is returning to a barren, eroded surface.

A pale-flowered ling, calluna vulgaris, peeks out from its sheltered den on an exposed tor.

Erica tetralix, the cross-leaved heath, holds high its tight cluster of flowers.

By late July the hillsides sing with colour as the heathers froth purple against the cool gray rocks and the fresh green of the blaeberry.

When it's crowded on the ground the heather happily adapts to rock-face living. Here on Ben Crom the normal purple and a rare white Bell Heather share a crevice.

Binnian's high tors watch over the Kingdom of Mourne.

While far below men crawl in clay and clod
Sublimely I shall stand alone with God.

MARY SINTON LEITCH

The upper slopes of the Pot of Legawherry

'The Rune and the Echo'

THE CLIMBERS:
'Now and tomorrow
O hill-gods grant us
The breadth of your vision
The calm of your vapours –
granite's stability,
heather's tenacity,
cataract's purity,
poise of your pinnacle
reaching to heaven'.

THE ECHO:
'Now and forever
our ways be unto you
challenge and conquest
stern and sufficing -
white peace of our snow,
grey grief in our rains,
flame of our sunsets
freedom of eagles – a dream in our dust'.

BRENDA G MACROW

In an almost biblical atmosphere, shafts of sunlight flare out
from Donard's brow as if to remind those toiling below that
St Patrick's disciple Domangard made this mountain a holy one.

Each cloud-capped mountain is a holy altar,
An organ breathes in every grove.

THOMAS HOOD

On Spence's Mountain

The stillness, the moonlight, the mystery,
I've bade 'em goodbye – but I can't.

ROBERT SERVICE

THE LIFE THAT LIVES ON MOURNE

THE BEAR has long gone, no wolf howls now from Altataggart's tor, the last wild boar fell centuries ago to the hunting spear. Now the red flash of a man-shy fox disappearing between Bearnagh's high rocks, or a ghostly winter-coated hare loping across the snow are likely to be the only reminders that we do not share the mountains just with sheep.

In the lower hills, where moorland fuses with wood and field and hedgerow, more animals live – mouse and vole, squirrel, badger and hedgehog, and, once again, warrens of rabbits that feed the stoat and the birds that swoop from rock and tree. Life is richer in the shelter here, but the world above of rock and bog, wind and cold, is only for those that can live on harsh terms.

The stripping away of their ancient woodland and scrub started a downward spiral of the diversity of life in the Mountains of Mourne that a deteriorating climate and grazing practices made irreversible.

As the soils lost their nutrients and acid bog spread, plants that demanded more than the mountains could now offer retreated down the slopes, and along with them went the animals and insects they fed. Seed-eating birds were left with poor pickings and the insect eaters with even less. There was no shelter from the mountain winds, except for those that lived down among the heather stems.

But although they provide a spartan diet, and those that feed there must stake out wide territories to meet their needs, the Mournes do offer a choice of habitats to which a select, but limited, range of normally lowland birds have adapted.

Circling high or soaring and tumbling between their lofty crags, like the very spirits of the rock at play, the ravens never leave their mountain home; in the silent winter theirs is the only voice to be heard on the wind. The peregrine falcons retain the remote eyries they have built but seek their winter food in the lower countryside around. Sometimes they enjoy the bonus of a 'meal on a wing' as scatterings of homing pigeon feathers testify.

The little wren, so vocal in the summer, stays on too, quietly sheltering in the rocks and heather, but harsh winters take a heavy toll. The bird that epitomises heather moor, the red grouse, is now almost a rarity,

The last wild boar to fall in Mourne? Sadly probably just from the carcase of a pig that never made to the abattoir.

It is reckoned that six sheep can live in the place of one cow but not only do sheep bite more closely and indiscriminately but they are more mobile than cattle and twenty-four pointed hooves do much more damage than four large hooves. Sheep have a depressing effect on flowering plants and shrubs, and indirectly on insect and bird life. Not only have they reduced tree-growth on the hill margins to a few stunted specimens of prickly thorn and holly, but they have accelerated the processes of peat erosion.

ESTYN EVANS – *MOURNE COUNTRY*

decimated by years of wet summers, disturbance and ill-managed burning. A visiting buzzard may sometimes startle, crashing out from high conifers, but not since 1836 has a golden eagle circled in majesty the peaks of Mourne.

The late mountain spring brings back the birds and their songs as the summertime residents spread back up from the lowlands to breed, the year's explosion of new insect life restocking their larder. Skylarks soar singing from the grassy slopes and the native meadow pipits, grey wagtails, stonechats and snipe are joined by the migrants from Africa, the wheatears and the ring ouzel. From the trees below, the sound of a cuckoo may occasionally carry up the hillside; sadly too seldom.

Many thousands of square feet of canvas have been covered over the decades by artists attempting to capture the essence of the Mournes. John Luke's playful but knowledgeably observed painting *In the Mournes* (1936) expresses the spirit of the mountains better than most.

The mountains lie in curves so tender
I want to lay my arm about them,
As God does.

OLIVE TILFORD DARGAN

Slieve Donard and companions in dawn mist

WATER

Cove Mountain stream leaps down from the high plateau it drains on its way to the Annalong River, then to join with the waters that will be piped from Silent Valley to Belfast.

'Mountain Burn'

I am the mountain burn. I go
Where only hill-folk know;
Pitter-patter, splash and spatter,
Goblin laughter, elfin chatter!
I am a chain of silver under the moon;
A spell that breaks too soon;
Lost voices chuckling across the peat.
Or faery feet
Echoing where the dancing harebells blow.

The silent places know me. Trees,
Stately and cool,
Gaze at their green reflection where I flow
Into some shadowy pool.
I am a ribbon of light, a flash of blinding
    white
Foam where the pale sun lingers
Over the heathery waste.
And still my long green fingers
Probe with a surgeon's skill the perilous
    grey
Slopes of the ferny gorge, to carve away
Granite and stone and bleached bone
To suit my changing taste.
I am brilliant as the stars, and timeless;
Sad as the earth, and strong
As mortal love. And through the long
Enchanted hours of sun and showers
I charm the hills with endless, rhymeless

Cadences of song.
Water the softest element after air,
has sculpted fantastic forms
out of the strewn boulders, frost fractured
    long since
and brought life down like landlocked
    meteors
in winter rages past, till now
all rough and raw-edged fragments are
    smoothed.

Water and the pull of the earth's far centre
have played the artist, moulded these
fantasies in stone, gothic and barbarous
but water the artist has many lifetimes!

BRENDA G MACROW

Streams

AN AWFUL lot of water falls onto the Mountains of Mourne. Sweeping 3,000 feet up from the sea and the low plains of Co Down they create their own winds, bring their own clouds – and it seems there is nothing they like more than a good soaking!

With an average rainfall of 50 inches – and passing 80 on some of the western high ground – even the 95 per cent water holding capacity of their peat blanket is stretched to its limits – and beyond.

The peat and its main constituent, the brightly coloured sphagnum mosses, form an effective natural flood-control system, absorbing millions of tons of water in the rainy times and releasing it gradually downslope over days or weeks to be drained away to the reservoirs and the sea by the streams whose constant chattering is cheerful company on every mountain walk.

For their area the Mournes boast an exceptional number of streams, now spilling and splashing in exuberance down stony cascades, now winding with deep clear stillness across peaty mountain terraces, joining with each other and then with others, gathering the waters from neighbouring hillsides as they grow to riverhood.

Crystal water and crystal rock, together shaping landscape; the streams sparkling in eternal youth as the mountains grow smooth and sage. Few places in the mountains are far from the sounds of the waters splashing down their stony courses, drumming into deep pools or gurgling unseen through the tunnels they carve through the peat. The streams are guides too; follow them up their busy ways and they can reveal some of the most exquisite secret places of the mountains, magic moss-fringed pools in many-hued rock, silver cascades in purple heather, never to be seen by the walker on the path.

The busy streams fill some ten rivers that through the valleys they themselves helped shape, drain the mountains, coiling away, twisted shining ribbons. Some like the lovely Shimna or Spence's River, have hardly bid the hills goodbye before they enter the sea, others ramble through miles of farmland, ducking under tracks and roadways, paying their respects to the fields and homesteads that greet them on their way. The longest, the River Bann, is born on the reedy slopes of Slieve Muck and takes their peat-filtered waters more than 100 miles to Ireland's northern coast, but most of the rain that washes Mourne returns to the ocean within sight of the hillsides on which it fell.

A vertical garden of emerald moss flourishes where a little stream trickles gently down over a smooth granite boulder.

A cool pool, the perfect end to a long hot day.

The very air one breathes among these hills
A panacea seems for human ills –
So by the borders of this purling stream,
Among the heather, let us rest and dream.

J W MONTGOMERY

'Summer Silence'

There's a pool in the valley,
Where two streams flow together,
Over it the mountains
Drowse in the sultry weather,
Silent the long green hollow,
Silent the shadowy glen,
No sound of the sheep on the hill,
Nor the labours of men.

Very slow, very still
The shrunken water run
Over their granite bed
Silvered by the sun,
And the water-music
Whispers less and less,
Not a voice, but the ghost of a voice
Haunting loneliness.

The valley will sleep thro' morning,
Thro' noon and afternoon,
Thro' the gossamer hour when evening
Leads forth a tawny moon.
Silent her delicate footsteps
Over the sky,
And silent as moon-lit heavens
Will the valley lie.

RICHARD ROWLEY

The Altataggart Stream silvers the granite of its deep chasm as it plunges into the Kilbroney Valley.

A *river's tale*

Mountain streams have fun, dancing and splashing down steep channels, meandering with deep calm where the ground gives them rest, plunging powerfully through steep gorges and into deep pools as their waters and strength increase, settling down to a sage and placid dignity when they leave mountain and forest.

This sequence of pictures shows the journey of the Cascade River, from its birth in the high ice-scooped corrie of Legawherry to the sea at Newcastle – down the undulating mountainside and through the forest of Tollymore, where the waters it gathers from the slopes of Slievenaglogh, Shanslieve and Slievenabrock mix with those that the Shimna and the Trassey rivers bring from the western valleys. Broad and strong now it flows gently towards the town, pausing before entering the sea to create the little boating lake that has brought delight to generations of visitors to the resort.

The lakes

ONCE THE chill waters of many lakes, big lakes, snow fed, lapped the slopes of the Mountains. Some lasted only centuries, some a few thousand years, before draining away with the breaching of the walls of ice and glacial debris which dammed them in. The torrents of silt-laden waters were so great that in places they gouged away the solid rock. Other lakes remained to be gradually filled in by sand and gravels washing off the mountain slopes and in time became peat bogs as millennia of accumulating plant remains shrank their shore lines.

Only two natural lakes worthy of the name still exist, Binnian Lough, on a high mountain platform, and Blue Lough in the valley below it, nestling under neighbouring Lamagan's protective ramparts. Three other once-broad lakes have become mere pools, almost swallowed by the encroaching peat. Shan Lough, still marked blue on the map, can be walked

(or squelched!) across, the second Blue Lough in the Mournes, now tiny, once filled the basin between Bearnagh and Doan where the layers of its ancient bed can be seen in the river cutting a kilometre away, and Cove Lough, described 250 years ago by traveler Walter Harris as '. . a beautiful lake, circular and clear as crystal', has almost disappeared into the rushes.

But proud peaks need shining water to admire themselves in and man has given back to the Mournes what the ages took away. The plunging, sinuous reservoir lakes of the Silent Valley, legendary and lovely Lough Shannagh, preserved as a beach-fringed lake by a little concrete dam across its outlet, and Spelga Reservoir, now rippling where deer and cattle once grazed, reflect for all the shapely curves and the changing moods of the mountain world.

Cradled in its high mountain platform Binnian Lough witnesses the endless cycles of seasons and weathers.

Lough Shannagh

Spelga Reservoir lies
placid in the mist.

Michael George Crawford – Lough Shannagh's Sprite

Lough Shannagh is a flash of light as a ray of sun penetrates the mist swirling around it.

After the coming of the Milesians the Mournes formed part of the possessions of the powerful Iranian clan O'Haidth but in the Twelfth Century the clan Aogus became lords of Iveagh and the MacMahons from Cremorne in Co Monaghan obtained a footing in Mourne and subsequently acquired the whole district, giving it their tribe-name and pushing back the O'Haidth who retired to the great mountain glen close to Lough Shannagh.

The clans at length became fast friends and the chief Mahon was soon a suitor for the hand of 'Sheelagh of Shannagh' the beautiful daughter of the chief of clan O'Haidth.

She was a fearless hunter, like a phantom rider on a phantom steed, but once when hunting a very swift fox she outdistanced her companions and did not notice that the Benns were being blotted out by a great white fog which was drifting through the valleys, obscuring everything in its way. She was so intent on

the pursuit that she did not know where she was until suddenly she found her horse was swimming in the enchanted waters of Lough Shannagh, and the fox had vanished as if by magic or as if the lake had swallowed him. The thick mist closed round her as she urged her steed, first in one direction and then in another, without being able to reach the shore. She became more and more bewildered and let the horse swim round in a circle until they went down together in the depths of the lake.

As the years passed the grief of the loss faded and the memory, except for shepherds' tales of a mystery lady on horseback riding the shores of the lonely lough. The 'Maid of the Mist' they called her.

On the tenth anniversary of Sheelagh's disappearance Chief Mahon was again hunting in the mountains with a party of his own clan when they started a beautiful white doe and gave chase, with Mahon in the lead.

The white doe sped away, through glens and mountain passes, closely followed by Mahon until his comrades were left far in the rear. Like a shadow the doe rushed up the steep sides of Slieve Bignion still followed by Mahon, but when he descended the next glen, which was wild and very long, the mountain mists again rolled down, shutting out every object, even the white doe.

He was lost but suddenly through the thick white mist he heard the sound of a pony's feet galloping over the turf, and soon the horse and rider bore down to him, and passed like a flash, but on the instant he saw the face of Sheelagh, pursuing the fox that had led her to her death. As she passed she looked him in the eye and the impulse to follow her seized him so strongly that he put spurs to his horse and flew through the fog in pursuit.

Out of the glen and up to the high plateau where lies Lough Shannagh the mist-maiden dashed, on across the very waters, and sank from sight. A low moaning came to Mahon's ears, a faint sound that swelled to a piercing cry of anguish. So real did it seem that he urged his horse out into the waters in a wild

attempt to save her. His courser made an awful bound as he plunged into the Lough, giving a cry of fear as if he knew both their lives were at stake.

When Mahon reached the fatal spot only the white doe was to be seen, swimming round in the swirling waters. Now it came closer and closer as the waves of fog thickened round them, and that was the last of Mahon. He was seen no more; gone to join his first-promised bride beneath the waters of the enchanted lake where she dwells as the white doe, under the 'Lord of the Lake' the magic Sionnach, the fox.

Lough Shannagh, the lake of myths and moods

New, shining lakes shine like mirrors among the peaks. The 1,700 million gallons of water that fill Ben Crom Reservoir began gathering in 1957 with the completion of the second high dam in the valley of the Kilkeel River. Cast in concrete the dam wall is strictly utility, but it does provide a handy way across the gorge!

Blue Lough nestles below the steep ramparts of Slieve Lamagan.

Nearly 50 years ago the berries shone red on these rowan trees on the slopes of the deep and steep valley of the Kilkeel River. Then the valley was dammed and the waters of the Ben Crom Reservoir rose and drowned them. Sometimes, when drought shrinks the lake, they return, gaunt skeletons on a bleached landscape.

But life never misses a chance. Within just days, the dried and cracked reservoir bed is sprouting new growth, destined though it is to have but a short time in the sun.

Great things are done when men and mountains meet;
This is not done by jostling in the street.

WILLIAM BLAKE

Climbing on Cove Mountain

MAN IN MOURNE
'A Training Day'

10.15 pm. The half-moon floated over Lamagan, to the west the tors of Bearnagh framed the last dying rays of the sun – below the Brandy Pad pointed to the artificial illuminations of Rathfriland. Sounds – few if one discounted the feeble breeze off Commedagh. Thoughts drift aimlessly back to morning – figures arrive at the door – yes – put your belongings there – stacks of gear – dixies – tents – stoves – food – ropes – helmets – more food – belts – chocs – into red – blue – green, neatly packed – crammed or stuffed – Joe Browns – Whillans – Auguilles – Cyclops – pack frames. Crocodile of names following through forest – over river – wet stones – wet boots – wet feet – sweating up hill – over wall – the Bogs of Slievenabrock – Pot of Legawherry – loose boulder on Slieve Coragh ridge sliding down – smell of sulphur and brimstone – white anxious faces peering up. Traverse the scree left to below – sinister – slimy – boulder-choked grassy gully – steep – grotty – nail breaking – rucsac-grabbing rock walls. The nearly serious mishap – stone dislodged – head injury – group reaction – decision deferring – on to camp under Beg.

Tension easing as the climb unfolds – steep – exposed – good runners – dry rock – boots working well. Belayed – all up – cameras clicking – down the Coach Road – 'Looks greasy' – 'Well protected – 'Worth trying' – 'Hell, it's foul'. Last move – 'Where's the ledge?' – 'OK, climbing' – 'Going well' – 'What next?' – 'I'm game' – 'Hate this first pitch' – 'Come on, steady up' – whip in an early runner – up right, finger hold good, change hands – lean over – good jug – step out – great, chock in – feel for the crack – 'Got it' – watch the loose stone here – onto the bulge, step up. On belay – 'Boy, that last pitch nearly got me' – 'Nice, wasn't it?' – 'Bit min in the middle' – 'Don't

like that layback bit' – bomb down to the camp – 'How'd it go?' – 'Wee buns' – cup of tea laced with brandy – 'Boy, if this is hell' he says.

Well, better move on, it's a good step home yet. All the road back wondering – is this what mountains and mountaineering mean: solitude – companionship, beauty – danger, enjoyment – suffering, relaxation – physical exhaustion?

TEDDY HAWKINS – FROM 'PEAK VIEWING', THE JOURNAL OF THE NI MOUNTAIN LEADER TRAINING BOARD, 1982

An early start for competitors in the 'Mourne Mountain Marathon' the annual two-day test of endurance and navigation skills which draws fell runners and fit walkers from all over Britain and Ireland. Restricted numbers and varied routes prevent environmental damage.

The paths

YOU FOLLOW in footsteps as ancient as human life in Ireland when you walk the tracks and paths that vein the Mountains of Mourne.

The trails of scuffed rock and raw peat that climb to the summits are young, the mark of leisured man, but still drawing the walker through the mountain fastness are the lines of the paths that were first etched by the silent feet of hunting man as he forayed through the wooded valleys and passes.

Later these tracks became the routes of easiest travel for the early farmers walking and trading between their stone-circled settlements on the cleared land on either side of the mountain barrier, for inland families to reach the coastal fisheries, and for their cattle to be taken to their summer pastures in the wide upland valleys.

The Trassey Track, probably the most walked path in the Mournes, leads under the glacier-sheared cliffs of Spellack.

Four thousand years ago prospectors, scouring Ireland for lodes of precious copper and tin for the first bronze age smelters, trod the tracks as they explored the seemingly promising granite outcrops of the Mournes. They found none and moved on, but generations later the stone men would widen and surface many of their ancestors' paths to extract the only wealth the mountains could offer – hard crystal granite for the roads and lintels and stern buildings of industrial Britain.

The hard-booted feet of other stone men, men from the lowland towns who over 18 summers climbed daily to build the 22 miles of massive wall that links the High Mourne summits, trod out different trails that even after three quarters of a century can still be followed.

Meanwhile through the centuries the layers of peat had been building as the mountains were stripped of their trees. When this peat came in turn to fuel the fires of a growing population other paths were widened to take the carts where wheels could go to the bogs. Where the ground was too rough and steep new deep tracks were carved by the wooden runners of the farmers' slipes (sleighs) piled with turf.

And interweaving with them all, of course, and draped like a web across all the hills, are the miles of seemingly aimless tracks made by the flocks of foraging sheep since the mountains were given to them 200 years ago. Sheep tracks are not always wise paths to take – sheep have a different agenda.

The Brandy Pad, for 8,000 years a 'high road' through the Mournes.

Oh how I long to travel back and tread again That ancient track.

HENRY VAUGHAN

Take a path and the path takes you. It flows with the energy of those who made it. Today the ancient tracks, some scrambling adventurously round the slopes, others wide and worn and purposeful, thrusting into the valleys, draw in those who walk now for pleasure, seeking the company of rock and stream. Those whose legacy they are, who first passed that way, the hunters, the farmers, the tinkers, the herdsmen, the stone men, the peat cutters, have long passed on.

Or might they not still walk with you their ancient ways?

The Glen River track to Donard and Commedagh

83

Leitrim, and a lone
figure takes the track
to Pierce's Bog.

'God's candle-sticks alight'

'The Travellin' Man'

Sez he, an him meetin' me
On a mountain track in Mourne,
It's not that I'm sae oul' Mister,
Only badly worn.
Hacked wi' the wind, Mister,
An' wrinkled wi' the sun,
A travellin' man,
An' his road near done.

My wife, sez she, what's ailin' ye?
Now, why can't you rest?
Ye're far too oul' for trampin'
The Mountains east an' west.
Sez I, a fret is in my feet,
To rammle an' to roam,
There's quiet in the mountains,
But a scoldin' tongue at home.

The hills I've tramped since I was young!
Each time I breast the rise,
I think I'll find a wonder, dawnin' in the skies.
Seven candle-sticks in Heaven
An' music in the wind;
It's miracles I'm lookin' for,
But what do I find?

A candle-stick in Heaven?
A new star in the blue?
A voice, a whisper from the clouds,
As everything turns new?
Och, none o' these; the same oul' hills,
The heather stretchin' wide,
The granite glintin' in the sun,
Nary a thing beside.

Trassey Track

Then down the hill I stumble,
An' take the dusty road,
Heavy is the goin',
An' weary is the load.
The dream is withered in my heart,
The song stilled on my tongue,
Och, differ'nt was the journey
The days that I was young.

But where there's mountain there is hope,
An' sometime, day or night,
I'll reach the lucky peak an' see
God's candle-sticks alight,
Flarin' out acrost the heavens,
Puttin' out the sun;
The travellin' man comes home at last,
His long road done.

RICHARD ROWLEY

85

'Bivouacs in the Mournes'

Thirty years ago bivouacs and other shelter stones were very popular with the walking and climbing fraternity. Probably the reason was the lack of lightweight equipment, and if you didn't have to lug a tent with you then so much the better. Such was the popularity of some of these spots that you had to arrive in good time to secure a place.

A favourite site was the Holly Tree. Just above the last bridge on the Glen River it provided sheltered haven at week-ends. Further up there was Camp Two on the right bank of the river at the boulder which marks the great swathe up to Eagle Rock. On bad nights it was the Ice House and in really severe weather, or a late arrival in Newcastle, the cellars of the now demolished Donard Lodge provided a welcome retreat.

The little hut at the exit from Lough Shannagh was always a popular spot, especially for functions, but perhaps the Hilton of the shelter stones was the big rock on the spur where the Mill River now meets the Ben Crom reservoir. Like many great

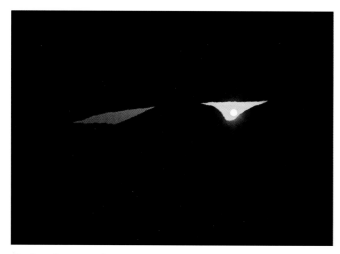

Shelter stone sunrise

institutions of the past it is rather seedy now. The entrance used to be built up with stones and the floor had a foot of fine dry heather. There was even a visitor's book made from a Scots Porridge Oats packet and spare paraffin and candles were always to hand. At one time it boasted a gadget called a volcano. This consisted of a hollow water jacket down which you stuffed heather, paper or anything remotely combustible. The roar as it rapidly heated the water amply justified its name.

The base of Lamagan, near the slabs, provided plenty of shelter stones. Unfortunately they were all rather small and most accommodated one or two people. For a social evening it was necessary to select a series of these within shouting distance of each other. Getting fed up with the yelling across a stiff breeze one night we decamped to Cove Cave. Although commodious it does tend to be a little draughty and the flattest spot is at about 45 degrees. Later we fixed up one of the old stone workers' bothies near Cove but it was never comfortable.

Bivouac equipment was rather basic. I had a sleeping bag made from two army blankets. Each one was sewn into a separate bag and heather was stuffed into the space between the inner and the outer. To do this required gathering vast amount of heather and assembling it, to the protests of one's companions, inside the shelter stone. The packing could only start when you were in the two bags and necessitated a deal of shoving, squirming and rolling about. The result was an enormous roly poly of doubtful stability and left the operator in a frazzle of sweat, and his companions muttering in anger.

Cooking utensils were of the simplest. A two pound fruit tin fitted with a wire was considered very avant garde. It had many advantages; it was light, cheap, dispensable and, when suspended on a crane over a few sticks could boil water in

Moonlit camp below Bearnagh

I live not in myself,
but I become
Portion of that
around me; and
to me
High mountains
are a feeling, but
the hum
Of human cities
torture.

GEORGE, LORD BYRON

minutes. On the minus side it did require a rather noisy technique to suck out the contents without getting burned on the lips.

If the cooking gear was simple then it was to match the food. Porridge formed a great part of the diet, often being tarted up with jam, honey, dried fruit or treacle. After the war ex-army compo rations were available for many years. Their contents varied although what was inside was not divulged until they were opened. It was a sort of lucky dip. The best one contained boiled sweets, a hard meat bar, pressed dried fruit, an oatmeal bar, one cigarette and a square of green toilet paper. I suppose with green the army didn't think you were surrendering!

BRIAN GIBSON 'BIVOUACS IN THE MOURNES' FROM PEAK VIEWING SPRING 1983

Shelter stone on Cove Mountain – very cosy, when it doesn't have a stream running through it!

THE STONES
Granite cubed

MAN SPLIT granite into blocks to build his cities; nature split granite into blocks to shape mountains. As the great volumes of magma cooled and turned to stone deep cracks split its outer layers, the layers from which the mountains were later carved. These fractures, criss-crossing each other, formed the distinctive pattern of vertical joints visible everywhere in the mountains and, providing channels for water and ice to penetrate the rock, played a major role in the shaping of the Mournes.

Millions of years of erosion later, only recently in the long life of the mountains, the removal of the entombing weight of overlying rock gave the mountain masses room to 'stretch'. A new set of fractures split the rock, this time parallel to its undulating surfaces and cutting across the ancient vertical fractures, splitting the rock into cubes and wide, curved sheets of granite. On the summits and in valley bottoms these slabs lie near to horizontal but on the valley sides they dip in line with the slopes, now forming in places plunging faces of bare rock.

The ease with which such slabs, especially in glacial conditions, can flake off and slide down the mountain sides, is a major factor in the shaping of smooth-domed granite hills. They make life simpler for stone cutters, hard for plant life and challenging for scramblers!

Poulaphouca, the Devil's Cauldron, is beautifully rugged. The Slievemore slope is exceedingly steep and covered with long screes of loose stone. On the opposite or Slieve Bearnagh side a series of great joint planes in the rock have produced bare slopes of granite of prodigious extent, on which neither plant nor animal may obtain a foothold.

ROBERT LLOYD PRAEGER – OFFICIAL GUIDE TO
COUNTY DOWN

V-diffs on Bearnagh slabs!

The hills are going somewhere;
They have been on their way a long time.

HILDA CONKING

Most of the summits are dome-shaped or conical,
as is usually the case with granite mountains; but
some of them, notably Slieve Bearnagh and Slieve
Bingian, are crowned with glorious crags, where on
the calmest day the wind sings through the crevices,
and rustles the shining leaves of the Dwarf Willow,
the Cowberry and other Alpine plants.

ROBERT LLOYD PRAEGER –
OFFICIAL GUIDE TO COUNTY DOWN

The great north tors of Binnian

Rock sculpture

NOT ALL the mountains of Mourne are crowned with tors, the towering megaliths that burst dramatically through the living skin of some summits, as if straining yet higher for the sky.

Small differences in the chemistry and structure of the five pulses of granite that built the mountains influence the way weathering shapes them. (Drilling has indicated a sixth granite lying deep beneath the High Mournes). The tors are the surviving cores of those granites whose upper layers, made porous by hot gases frothing through them as they hardened, rotted in times of warmth and moisture. They were left standing proud when the days of ice returned and the decayed material around them was carried away downhill.

The highest of the mountains, Slieve Donard and neighbouring Slieve Commedagh, do not wear crowns; commanding presence needs no frills. Broad and rounded, their summits have been slowly shaped from the oldest and toughest of the granites, defying erosion and resistant to weathering.

The crested majesty of Slieve Binnian and Slieve Bearnagh on the other hand are the finest displays of tor development in Ireland. Their crenellated summit ridges form distinctive skylines that beautifully counterpoint the smoothed brows of their sisters and reward the walker with the experience of being among great sculptures – Moores, Hepworths, that invite an exploring, caressing hand.

Nature shows its sense of humour too in its sculpting of the tors and the massive loose boulders that lie around them. Working on the jointed granite it has created a fun collection of fantasy human heads and animal shapes for the imaginative to find and enjoy.

Mountains are good to look upon,
But do not look too long,
They are made of granite,
They will break your heart.

GRACE HAZARD CONKLING

Bearnagh's southern ramparts

Granite shows its lighter side

The 'G2' granite (as it is excitingly called by geologists) from which these tors were mostly carved surged up just a short time after the first one had hardened. Deeper and slower to cool, it is coarser and where bubbles of its hot gasses were trapped underneath the solid rock above it they created cavities in which perfect crystals of amethyst and smokey quartz, feldspar, mica, beryl and topaz could develop. In a few places, where the meeting of the granites is now exposed on the hillsides – as at the 'Diamond Rocks' north east of Hare's Gap – these gems could once be readily found, but generations of amateur geologists and professional collectors have left them a rare treasure. The sharp eye however can still strike lucky when a sparkle might signal a fine cluster emerging form the receding peat that covers the glacial gravel.

The Castles of Commedagh, the Gothic rampart of buttresses and crumbling gulleys low down on the south side of the mountain, is a demonstration of weathering in action, with the winter frosts prying off particles that wash down the slopes in drifts and with jointed pillars, tors in miniature, emerging from the receding surfaces. This same feature is mirrored on the opposite side of the mountain at the head of the ice-scooped Pot of Legawherry. The precipitous gorge of the Mill River flowing into Crom Reservoir has been gouged out through the same vulnerable stone.

Ironically it was this same granite, but from its deeper, protected layers, that provided the finest of stone for building and polishing and which has been most extensively quarried on the lower slopes.

The perceptive walker on tracks that lead to places where the pale gray stone of Mourne was quarried may sometimes spot interesting fragments of jet black granite. Sadly for the budding geologist in search of exciting discovery these do not come from hidden veins of exotic rock! Polished black tomb-stones once much in demand could not be obtained from the Mournes so the granite for them was imported from Africa and other places. On their way to the local quarries the lorries carried up waste chippings from the yards and used them to build up the tracks, so granites from around the world lie together.

There is a fresh palette for the start of each new mountain day.

Looking over the Silent Valley from Ben Crom

The rising midwinter
sun paints the
south-eastern sky.

*Night's candles are burnt
Out, and jocund day
Stands tiptoe on the
Misty mountain tops*

WILLIAM SHAKESPEARE

93

The harvest of stone

THE GRANITE mountains, with their shroud of peat and leached gravels, can provide scant sustenance for plant or animal, but their hardness filled the plates of many an impoverished family through lean times.

The boulders that litter the slopes in their millions and the slabs of exposed living rock provided a crop that helped the population of some foothill townlands to actually increase following the famine years while much of the surrounding county was being depopulated.

But hard granite gives a hard living. Patches of age-darkened spals (spoils – waste chippings) chink underfoot across wet, wind-swept mountainsides to mark where boulders were split and chiselled into square setts, making the difference for many between survival and destitution. Little roofless windbreaks, sometimes in clusters where a rockface fed a number of families, abandoned rocks edged with punch-holes, bear silent witness everywhere to the strength, skills and endurance required of men who reaped harvests of kerbstones and lintels.

At one time five ships sailed from Annalong Harbour every week loaded with stone for the streets and buildings of Liverpool and Lancashire. Countless thousands more tons of quarried stone took the road to Belfast, building its foundation as an industrial and trading city.

Boulders ice-plucked from the mountains and strewn across the countryside had been providing ready building materials since the first megaliths were rolled and levered into position to create great tombs and to stand to mark the sacred places. They made strong circular walls to protect iron-age farmsteads and later a stern religion used granite to build stern grey churches for its faithful and to mark their graves.

Being worked on an industrial scale left the hillsides bearing many scars. The hundreds of small hand-worked sites, once stark white with fresh-chipped stone, have been weathered by time and nature to blend back into the natural background of heather-fringed dark rock. No longer disfiguring they now add new features of interest to be stumbled on along remote tracks, poignant reminders of a busy mountain past.

Slidderyford portal grave. Five thousand years ago the pre-bronze age peoples, used the great granite blocks the mountains had shed to preserve the remains of their revered ones and define their territory.

94

Slower to heal are the great quarried bites that were opened later by machines with the power to take stone in huge blocks, spilling screes of wasted rock down the hillsides. Their Gothic walls of granite nakedly exposed, sometimes clothed in surreal sheets of colour by the primitive algaes that live where water streams down from the peat above, are forlorn places especially when the dark mists swirls, yet with a haunting fascination of their own, as if to offer some recompense for a desecration.

Only a little stone, more discretely quarried, is taken now. It is ironic but fitting that its last use on a grand scale was in the Mournes themselves where stone cut from the mountains was dressed to build the walls, embankments and buildings of the Silent Valley Reservoir. Created in a landscape with stone which was literally a part of it, here man has given back to the mountains a place of beauty in return for what he took away. There could be no more eloquent tribute to the elegance and strength of granite for the works of man – or a more appropriate memorial to all the men who ever worked it.

The Silent Valley

Living abstractions on a stone
canvas – Bloody Bridge quarry

*The entire Mourne range may be said to be one
unbroken mass of granite. At present but two
quarries tap this well nigh inexhaustible supply, a
fact greatly to be deplored, as the quality of the
granite is of the highest order – pronounced by
experts to be unrivalled of its kind.*

FROM *BEATTY'S GUIDE TO NEWCASTLE*, 1906

Croc-an-roe quarry

'Binnian Quarry'

A thousand men, a hundred years
Have prised and dug,
Have levered, sweated, feathered, punched
At this great quarry face,
And down the bouldered track
On Croc-an-roe
Have dragged and slipped

The sequined granite slabs
To kerb the streets of Liverpool,
To make and mend the twisting roads below,
To face the lesser stone of city towers,
To edge the tomb and mark the resting place
Of many a man who never looked on
Mourne.

J S DORAN

Walk through the mountains almost anywhere in Mourne, scramble under some precipitous rock-wall where you might well imagine that you are the first person ever to have trod, and the chances are that you will see the tell-tale marks of the stone-mason's jumper holes. The disused and overgrown tracks that wind up the slopes are of his making, floored with granite chips and levelled by the passage of slipe and stone-cart. Here and there you will come across the ruins of a stone-built forge where the men sheltered and sharpened their tools. There will be a working bench at the back opposite the door, with the marks of the fire alongside, and probably a hollowed tempered stone or 'fizz-trough' near the door.

ESTYN EVANS – *MOURNE COUNTRY*

Remains of a stone-mason's shelter near Lamagan. The hollowed 'fizz-trough' in the doorway held water to cool the red-hot metal tools during sharpening.

Split and shaped but never harvested, granite kerb-stones lie on the mountain side.

Arable land is almost absent on the Mourne slopes,
and the crops available consist of paving blocks
and kerbs, which are chiefly obtained by breaking
up the immense blocks of granite which are found
strewed over the valleys in great profusion.

FROM THE ITINERARY OF AN EXCURSION TO THE MOURNES
BY MEMBERS OF THE INCORPORATED GAS INSTITUTE,
JUNE 1898

Ageless granite walls create a unique pattern of tidy farmlands around the mountain feet.

It is a fact that before the old-timers in Mourne could claim to be farmers at all they simply had to be granite workers. To make fields they had to clear the moors where the heavy clay was as full of boulders as a chocolate bar is full of nuts. The reclaiming of the foothills meant the difference between a have and a have-not.

The rocks were 'riz' (raised), split on the spot into sizes that could be drawn to the borders of the new plots and built, loosely but permanently, into stone ditches for our little fields that, as you approach the foothills, get smaller and smaller. The stone ditches are a feature of the Mourne landscape, netting the whole uplands and mountain slopes, where they divide pasture from pasture. It has been estimated that we have 15,000 fenced fields and all are a lasting memorial to the mountainy men of Mourne.

J S DORAN – MY MOURNE

The Wall

UNCERTAIN NAVIGATORS bless it, wilderness purists deplore it and a million lunches have been eaten in its sheltering lee.

The men who spent 18 years creating it, men with 'powerful shoulders and hands like shovels', called it The Black Dike but within memory it has been The Mourne Wall, or simply The Wall; no one ever has to ask 'Which wall?'.

A bold territorial statement conceived in the closing years of Victorian assertiveness, it never served any practical purpose, a grandiose folly soaring and swooping for 22 miles with breaks only for a few gates and the odd vertical step along its route. Head height and three feet wide, it contains almost two million cubic feet of granite, more than 140,000 tons of stone skilfully fitted into place after being shaped from the boulders littering its course or, where these ran out, prised from the solid rock.

The Wall romps in a great circle from peak to peak of the High Mournes, built to enclose 9,000 acres of mountainside whose streaming waters are held captive in the Silent Valley and Ben Crom reservoirs before being sent to quench the human and industrial thirsts of Belfast.

Its builders were men of rock, farmers of a stony land who had to be fit to work granite as well as soil. From spring to autumn each year between 1904 and 1922 they climbed the mountains to build their Black Dike, adding almost a mile and a quarter to its length every year – a prodigious average of 50 feet of wall a day!

During the summer those who had furthest to walk camped under sail-cloth beside the wall, dropping down home mid-week for fresh supplies of eggs, butter, soda bread and tea and maybe porridge so thick it could be taken back up the mountain in slices.

They carried their seven-pound hammers and other iron tools up the mountains, they carried bags of coal and wood for the fires to sharpen their stone-punches and, for the towers on Donard, Commedagh and Meelmore, bags of sand and cement. They built the faces of the wall of rough-hewn, interlocking blocks, packed the centre with smaller stones and chippings and sealed it with two-hundredweight capstones, sliding them up sloping planks into place. They built a wall to last a thousand years.

The Wall

The Wall – running for 22 miles around High Mourne by summit and saddle

Each year the work of building the wall began in the month of March and after three months on the mountain the stone-men were as hard as steel. Quitting time came at the end of the week after the gang boss measured up how much of the wall had been built and then the boys grabbed their coats and never stopped running till they reached Annalong! Work finished on the wall when the light began to fade about mid-October.

W H CARSON – *THE DAM BUILDERS*

At strategic spots, 'sheep holes' were left in the walls to allow animals to pass through.

The millstones

MORE THAN 1,750 feet up on the northern ridge of the Mournes, where the ground starts to rise to the summit of Slievenaglogh, lies a massive memorial to generations of men whose strength and toughness must have equalled that of the rock from which they wrested a hard, hard living.

Once on the surface, cut from the living granite that here is exposed in horizontal slabs, but now almost buried by maybe a century of accumulating peat and heather, is a great pierced disc, a millstone, shaped by hand and chisel and then, mysteriously, abandoned, never to turn in the corn-mill for which it had been destined.

Six feet in diameter and the spindle hole cut through its centre showing it to be a foot thick, at the density of granite it weighs more than two tons, even carved almost to its finished shape to minimise its weight

The great millstone on Slievenaglogh

before the long haul by rope and slipe down the rough mountain slopes to a mill somewhere miles away.

Why did it never make that journey? Did death or change of fortune strike the man who daily climbed the hill to carve it or the moneyed one who ordered it to be made, or did new technology make the great stone redundant – as pre-cast concrete later sounded the death-knell of hand-shaped granite kerb-stones and lintels, hundreds of which also now lie, lichen-skinned, around the quarried hillsides, neatly stacked, waiting for the slipe that never came.

Four kilometres due east of the Slievenaglogh, and much more accessible to road and ship, is a hill actually called Millstone, from which these vital items were sent to grind the harvested oats and barley in townlands around Ireland and across the water. Most were carved from quarried slabs but one stone cut from the granite on the surface still lies just below the summit. Smaller than the great stone on Glogh and just roughly shaped, it lies where it was cut in a circle from the parent rock with a precision that looks as if it could be replaced with the joint being hardly visible.

But polished Mourne granite was a valued item of trade and widely sought after for turning grain into flour from long before powered mills were built requiring great stones. Granite querns for hand grinding have been found many miles away at excavated settlement sites from long before the time of the Normans.

THE HERITAGE
The silent testimonies

Dawn on Donard – The Summit Cairn on Donard was, before its destruction, a passage grave, possibly built, as at Newgrange, so that the light of the mid-winter sunrise shone into its inner chamber.

The Bronze Age North Cairn on Donard. The stone circle is modern, built by the author in memory of a sadly missed friend, who was also a friend of the Mournes.

The elder ones

FIVE AND a half thousand years ago the new immigrants, the first settled communities, with cultivated cereals and domesticated animals, spread out from their landing places on Carlingford Lough along the flanks of the Mountains of Mourne. With stone and bone they cleared and cultivated patches of the well-drained middle land between the swampy, densely covered low ground and the steep, thickly-wooded mountain wilderness, the lair of wolf and bear, but one where deer, hare, wild pig and a rich bird life rewarded the skilled hunter.

Cattle became the mainstay of life in Ireland, the foundation of wealth and influence, and families spent the summer months herding them on the upland pastures, but no permanent settlements were ever established in the high hills. The mountain fastness was the territory of the hunter and the woodsman, and a safe refuge for the outcast, the outlaw and those fleeing successive invaders.

Settled and secure on the cleared land around the Mournes the later neolithic farming tribes marked and sanctified their territory by building a great passage-tomb for their revered ones on the highest point of its highest mountain and two thousand years later their bronze-age descendants piled stones over the bones of their chieften into another high cairn nearby, on Donard's northern brow. The ravaged remnants of these tombs, and lesser ones on Commedagh and the hills overlooking Carlingford Lough, Slievemartin and Knockshee, are the only testimony the high mountains bear to 5,000 years of human life swirling around them.

When iron made men better at farming and fighting, when the new Gaelic culture and language spread through the land and, later, the new religion took over the ordering of their lives, men of substance around the mountain flanks built rings of high stone to protect their people and their stock. Encircling the mountains like a necklace these cashels in some cases grew in importance to become feudal citadels, and even, such as Kilmeloge below Slieve Binnian, ecclesiastical centres of influence.

In the 19th century, land hunger drove people further into the mountain valleys to seek a living, building strong stone houses to beat the mountain

Nature reclaims the stones of Kilmeloge, the iron-age cashel slumbering among the pastureland under Binnian. Kilmeloge is believed to have been the royal residence of Mourne, Cathair Boirche, before the conversion of its occupants, when it became a centre for the spread of Christianity under St Moluainen.

Still standing after a millennium and a half, the chancel arch of St Mary's Church keeps vigil over the narrow pass between mountain and sea, beside the Bloody Bridge River. It marks the first, and unsuccessful, attempts by St Patrick's disciples to expand Christian influence southwards into the reclusive Kingdom of Mourne.

winds. Today the people have gone, only the eternal winds move through their roofless homes and sheep graze the cultivation ridges that mark their labours and their dreams.

A little patch of daffodils returns still to bloom each spring far up the valley of Spence's River, which flows south west from deep in the mountains. Brought up from the low lands and planted – how many generations ago? – by a young wife, a mother, to splash their brightness and their hopes of spring against the dark cold walls of her family's home, they faithfully keep their yearly promise – but no one now is there to welcome them.

Carr's Cottage

IN THE 19th century many one-roomed homes were built on the mountain margins, their occupants facing years of backbreaking work digging out granite boulders to create fields and feed growing families. Many were abandoned after just one generation of uneven struggle, others in time were improved by those who found a measure of prosperity.

This 'wee humble cottage', the home of the Carr family by Spence's River, was photographed by Robert Welch in the 1890s. About the lives of many at the time it says everything.

Three decades later a larger, finer dwelling was built of cut granite blocks and roofed with slate. The old cottage was retained as an outhouse at its gable end. This way it remained for another 70 years. Surrounded with trees and with its front 'yard' levelled it is recognisable in the upper picture, right, only by its huge granite 'corner stone' on which the children were playing when Welch took his photograph.

This old cottage's fate, however, was not to crumble away like so many others – a new century, and a new owner, saw the main house being restored and the old cottage once again became a human habitation. Its walls raised to two-storeys it is now the ground floor of a modern extension to the house. And the 'big stane' is still there, waiting for children of the future to clamber on it once again.

Long roofless and overgrown, this now is the little house on the hillside, on the extreme left of the Robert Welch picture on p.110. This house, modest in size but built with all the skill of the stoneworker-farmer, was home to the McGoldrick family. Eleven children were born within its walls but the scourge of TB took seven, one by one, before they finished their childhood. The four who lived to become young adults took the only route open to so many, the ship to America, never to return. Their parents lived on through old age, the land was sold and the house was left to its memories and the wind.

Only a moldering wall among the trees of Tollymore forest now remains of an ancient Mourne home.

'An Irish Mother'

A wee slip drawin' water,
Me ould man at the plough,
No grown-up son nor daughter,
That's the way we're farmin' now.
'No work and little pleasure'
Was the cry before they went,
Now they're gettin' both full measure,
So I ought to be content.

Great wages men is givin'
In that land bayant the say,
But 'tis lonely – lonely livin'
Whin the childher is away,
Och, the baby in the cradle,
Blue eyes, and curlin' hair,
God knows I'd give a gra'die
To have little Pether there;
No doubt he'd find it funny
Lyin' here upon me arm,
Him – that's earnin' the good money
On a Californy farm.

Six pounds it was, or sivin
He sint last quarter day,
But 'tis lonely – lonely livin'
Whin the childher is away.

God is good – none bether,
And the Divil might be worse.
Each month there comes a letther
Bringing something for the purse.
And me ould man's heart rejoices
Whin I read they're doin' fine,
But it's Oh! To hear their voices,
And to feel their hands in mine.

The lucky horseshoe is no match for a hard economy.

To see the cattle drivin'
And the young ones makin' hay,
'Tis a lonely land to live in
Whin the childher is away.

Whin the shadders do be fallin'
On the ould man there an' me,
'Tis hard to keep from callin'
"Come in childher, to yer tea!"
I can almost hear them comin',
Mary, Kate and little Con –
Och, but I'm the foolish woman,
Sure they're all grown up and gone.

That our sins may be forgiven,
An not wan go astray,
I doubt I'd stay in Heaven
If them childher was away.

PERCY FRENCH

113

'Stone'

A roofless house makes a fine container for an opportunistic rowan.

Stone-filled window frame

Arcadia was never here,
Ice-needles tortured the thin soil,
spring snow lay long by the north wall,
yet the peat-fire had a summer heart.
Waves of life receding left
jetsam of stone – grey megaliths
half sunk in tussocky grass now
but still processional on the ridge above,
leading into a mystery:
In a cranny of the valley, a ring of stones
that sheltered a hearth once, a roofless hut
under the shadow of cairned hills.
The rushes cut each autumn
to mend the thatch, one year
were cut no more; over the centuries
the path was lost. Only stone lasts here.
Stone proclaims life, affirms a future
by virtue of so many pasts,
yet baffles questioning. As I touch walls
warm in the sun today, and feel
so many summers gentle to my hand
and yet withheld, I would crush stone
in my fist, if I could, till truth's milk ran.

RUTH BIDGOOD

A future from the past

NESTLING COSILY among the granite-walled fields that spread between Binnian's steep slopes and Kilkeel is Hanna's Close*, one of the last surviving clachans in Northern Ireland, relics of a medieval way of life. Until a decade ago crumbling into dereliction the 17th century Hanna's Close has been given new life, sensitively refurbished to retain its original features yet with modern facilities to provide unique and comfortable accommodation for visitors to Mourne. Run by the local development association, the listed and award-winning Hanna's Close is a superb example of successful rural regeneration, pointing a way ahead for communities facing declining farming livelihoods. Encouragement of such community projects and of farm diversification schemes such as provision of parking and accommodation facilities for hill-walkers is central to the tourism development strategy for Mourne.

*'Close' is the Scots version of clachan, small clusters of cottages occupied by related families under the ancient system of shared ownership of land. The word occurs in a number of places around the Mournes and indicates the origin of many of those living there.

Booley huts

A GHOSTLY RUSTLE of wind through the long grass, and the chatter of the stream busy nearby are today the only sounds to be heard at the little oases of green to be seen throughout the heathered slopes of the Mourne valleys.

But these swards, where no heather grows even after 150 years, once echoed to the sounds of the young people of the surrounding townlands as they lived through the long days of herding the wealth of their people, their cattle, taken each year to the upland pastures for summer grazing – the ancient farming practice of booleying.

The booley sites have lain silent since farm fields were enclosed and sheep took over the mountain slopes in the early nineteenth century. The walls of their primitive summer cabins, rebuilt each spring of turfs and thatched with branches and heather through which the acrid smoke of the cooking fire filtered away, have melted back into the earth leaving just low, often barely discernible, ridges which still allow their outline and doorways to be traced.

No great stones mark the antiquity of these humble remains but ancient they are and vital they were to the survival of the local farming families through all the ages and eras of Irish history. The sites were summer homes to uncounted generations since Neolithic farmers first cleared and occupied them, grazing their cattle, churning butter for food and barter, while the summer crops ripened on their unfenced fields below.

A booley hut site in the Rocky River Valley. Around the Mournes the remains of many such summer dwellings can be seen, melting back into the earth, reminders of a way of life going back to Neolithic times.

Booley cabins were built beside streams, on level ground, and with a wide view of the slopes over which the cattle roamed. The lush grazing above and around Spelga was the most important booleying ground for the farmers west of the Mournes but their summer homes now lie beneath the waters of the latter-day reservoir. Their times and lives are marked, however, in the names they gave the hills around – Butter Mountain, and Slievenamiskan (Sliabh Meascan), the hill of the butter store.

The remains of many booley houses can be found along the banks of the streams tumbling from the great Pot of Legawherry down to Tollymore, and in valleys opening above the southern plains. But by the stream running off Rocky Mountain, deep in the Western Mournes, a veritable deserted village lies slumbering. There the outlines of more than twenty house sites can be traced, a cluster of remains of many ages – but still just the last, topmost layer of a line of life that goes back to the dawn of farming.

Deer's Meadow (called by some King's Meadow because people have their grazing in it free), is resorted to by great numbers of poor people in the summer months to graze their cattle; they bring with them their wives, children and little wretched furniture, erect huts and live there for two months and sometimes more, and often cut their turf to serve for the next returning season, which done, they retire with their cattle to their former habitations.

ORDNANCE SURVEY MEMOIR OF SOUTH DOWN, 1834

The great summer grazing grounds of Deer's Meadow now hold the waters of Spelga Reservoir.

Booley hut sites high in the Cascade River valley

Altataggart Mountain

The 'holy sign' carved into the granite altar stone below Altataggart. Above it an area of sloping rock was cut away to provide a level surface on which to stand the candles and vessels for the clandestine Mass.

'Altataggart'

In the wood o' the priest
'Mid larch and pine,
Stands a boulder carved
With the holy sign;
And overhead
The pine and larch
Weave a green cathedral arch.

Thro' Altataggart
Goin my lone,
The candles gleamed
On the altar-stone;
And as the torrent's
Waters fell,
Came the sound of the Sacring-bell.

In Altataggart, the holy wood
Was filled with prayers
Of a multitude;
All unseen,
Beneath the trees
The folk of the valley,
Were on their knees.

Long years have passed
Since they knelt there,
Silence of Centuries
Shrouds their prayer;
But thro' the wood,
As I went my lone,
The candles gleamed
On the altar-stone.

RICHARD ROWLEY

The sward of soft moss seems to reflect the bright green of the larch bursting into new leaf above in Batt's Wood on Altataggart.

Mists and myths

The ancients left few marks of their being among the Mountains of Mourne but names still linger, flitting in the mists between history and myth – Slainge, Boirche, CuChulainn even fabled Finn McCool. The Formarians, the Fir Bolg, the legendary Milesians all came, made footprints, and passed on, leaving just folk memories. Why question them?

Slainge, prince of the Partholans, a people of Grecian origin who brought bronze to Mourne, was buried under the great north cairn on the highest of the mountains. It became his memorial and for two thousand years Sliabh Slainge was its name until Patrick's disciple Domangard (Donard) adopted the summit as his saintly retreat, bestowing holy status on it, and in time his name.

Where CuChulainn made his stand –
the mountains beyond Carlingford Lough.

But for almost ten centuries Beanna-Boirche, the Peaks of Boirche, was the name by which all the mountain range was known. Boirche, a royal prince, made South Down his territory around 250 AD. He and his successors had the honorary title of Cow Herd to the High King of Ulster, with the duty of protecting the cattle during their summer sojourn on the grassy slopes of the mountains. Folklore has it that Boirche was buried on Slievenamiskin overlooking the wide grazing grounds of Spelga, but his time came after that of the great cairns and no stone marks his bed. On the western brow of Slievenaglogh, however, you can sit on a great granite throne, from which he surely must have watched over the spreading lands below.

One of the first visitors to Boirche's new domain was the great Finn MacCumhail (Finn McCool), founder and leader of the third century militia force Fianna Erin. When not protecting the High King's interests Finn would lead his knights in great hunting expeditions throughout Ireland, and there are few mountain regions that do not have a hill, a glen or a rock bearing his name. During a foray into the Mournes his entourage made camp on the dry ground between the rich wooded valleys of the Annalong and Spence's rivers – the ridge now called Seefin (Suidhe-finn) – Finn's resting place.

It was towards the end of the 12th century that the mountains became the territory of a clan from the ancient and once powerful Mughdhorna (Mourne) people of Monaghan and Omeath. Squeezed out of their lands by more powerful tribes and plundering

Normans they moved away north-east to make a new home on the coastal plain behind the sheltering mountain barrier. They created a new kingdom but brought to it their ancient name, the name it bears still.

It was on the mountains on the south side of Carlingford Lough, the epic saga of the Cattle Raid of Cooley, recounts that the greatest of the Irish Heroic Age heroes CuChulainn single-handedly held off the forces of Queen Medb of Connaught for a whole winter to give Ulster time to muster troops and repel her invasion. But it was to the depths of Beanna-Boirche that CuChulainn retreated when, defeated by the warrior Conrigh in a fight over a woman, he suffered the shame of having his long hair, his sign of nobility and manhood, cut off. He lived for a year in seclusion far up the Silent Valley, hidden away from the eyes of men, until it grew and he could hold his head high once again. (Before CuChulainn adopted this Celtic name in later life he was called Setanta and it is possible that 'Silent' is a corruption of this word, the valley having been named after him.)

Over so many centuries the Mournes must have been a retreat of outlaws and refugees and frontier territory between scrapping, cattle-raiding, tribes so it is surprising that (with the exception of the 'Bloody Bridge' which marks the slaughter of a group of prisoners of the 1641 rebellion) none of the mountain place-names recall dirty deeds or bloodshed, events which would normally linger long in folk-memory. The loveliest of Mourne's rivers, the Shimna, is said to have run red in AD 703, however, after a great battle on Moneyscalp Hill, just north of Tollymore, in which the Ulidians defeated raiding

The vastness of the Silent Valley, where CuChulainn sought refuge for a year while his hair grew to mannish length again, lies now under the deep waters of the Ben Crom Reservoir.

Boirche's chair on Slievenaglogh looks over the grazing lands of Ulster

Danes. A deep gulley on the hill was filled with the dead and for centuries the stream running through what is now the Park's Azalea Walk to join the Shimna was known as the Sru-na-fola – the stream of blood.

Farming the land

'The Goat of Slieve Donard'

*I saw an old goat on the slope of Slieve
   Donard,
Nibbling daintily at the herb leaves that grow
   in the crevices,
And I thought of James Stephens –
He wrote of an old goat within my
   remembering.
Seven years ago I read –
Now it all comes back
Full of dreaming black beautiful crags.*

*I shall drink of the white goat's milk,
The old white goat of Slieve Donard,
Slieve Donard where the herbs of wisdom
   grow,
The herbs of the secret of life that the old
   white goat has nibbled,
And I shall live longer than Methuselah,
Brother to no man.*

PATRICK KAVANAGH

No more roaming and grazing the open hillsides now for the cattle of Mourne.

Dogs get more lucky!

It is a pleasure to stroll along the loanins between the granite walls, in the assurance that the gates will open easily and close securely, for the stone-worker must know how to work iron, and he takes a pride in the well-hung gates and farmyard fittings.

ESTYN EVANS –
MOURNE COUNTRY

As varied as the man and nature can make them – a selection of gate and fence fixtures from around the Mournes

Beneath the mountains

Their lives bounded by mountain and sea the people of Mourne have learned and lived by the laws of two contrasting worlds and created a culture unique in Ireland. Above: Annalong harbour below Slieve Binnian; opposite above: Newcastle beach; opposite below: Newcastle viewed from Slieve Donard; overleaf: the Annalong Valley from Ben Crom

Two voices are there; one is of the sea
One of the mountains; each a mighty voice.

WILLIAM WORDSWORTH

Newcastle – a sprightly little village – exceedingly well adapted as a watering place. The sea water is pure and strong, without any admixture of fresh water, and the beach, of the finest sand, is safe and admirably suited to the softer sex.

J B DOYLE 'TOURS IN ULSTER' 1854

Shimna River flowing through Tollymore

Sights such as this used to be common in some areas of the Mournes. Effort, enlightenment and education have virtually eliminated them but vigilance will always be necessary.

Litter picked up by the author along the way over the course of one year – about 30 walking days.

THE DUTY OF CARE

BY FELLING their trees, splitting their rocks, impounding their water, digging their peat, grazing their slopes, building their stones into walls and etching his pathways through them man, in his brief time in the long life of the Mountains of Mourne, refashioned their scenery.

The diversity of the life they are home to, the patterns of plant and rock and water, of forest, field and fenceline, are the legacy of the generations of his stewardship. He took from the mountains in his need and the imperative of livelihood left a changed landscape, the one in which his descendants now seek and find different riches.

Today the granite builds men and women, not the walls and footpaths of their cities. Coming to touch mountains they free their spirit, refresh their minds, test their resolve, learn of themselves.

Learn too why the mountain world, with all its beauties, challenges and magic moments, is to be cherished and protected, that such gifts will not be lost for themselves or for those who will follow. Learn that in damaging the mountain worlds they diminish the birthright of their children.

Man takes less from the mountains now – water, a little stone, grazing for his sheep. Thoughts of hydro-electricity schemes or more dammed valleys have rightly withered, quarrying is more discreet, the spaded bogs are left to heal themselves. The skirts of forest and parkland and smooth green fields have by

Treat the earth well.
It was not given to you by your parents,
It was loaned to you by your children.

MASAI PROVERB

their contrasts enhanced the noble ruggedness of the hills.

More come now than ever came for stone or peat but the walker who cares leaves no sign of his passing. The tramping boot, if thought guides it, need not bruise or wound where it steps. Rock was made to bear the touch of foot and hand, the plant perishes under 'the tourist's desecrating tread'.

The litter of the few who have not been taught to care remains an affront only as long as it is left to lie there by those who later pass by.

The Mournes have many scars to show for providing men with livelihood and sport. There need be no more. But the enduring mountains can be forgiving of mistakes; man is passing through and it is the quality of his own world he damages most by them. To the mountains the wounds are superficial, there will be time enough to heal them, and infinite time beyond.

Unperturbed, the Mountains of Mourne ponder their deep, slow secrets. One day, from the north, the ice will come again.

On a Personal Note

MY OWN first meeting with the Mountains of Mourne was at about the age of 10. My parents had taken a bungalow in Newcastle for a fortnight's holiday – with the thrill of a steam train trip from Belfast thrown in. It was a beach and gentle promenade holiday but on one day my father, who had never been on a mountain before (and never was again!) thought something a bit more adventurous was in order. The two of us took the Glen River track up through the forest, with majestic Donard in our sights. We investigated the old ice house where the forest gives way to the moorland and Donard didn't seem too high at all. After half an hour of summer heat, leg-abrading heather and boulders it seemed less of a good idea but, intrepid, we toiled on until at last we breasted the summit – of Thomas's Mountain, a mere foothill! Deceived by our optimism – as so many others have done before and since – we stood aghast at the sight of the real Donard, aloof, majestic and impossibly high above us still, and retreated in ignominy. (But Donard likes to toy with his visitors. In fact at that stage you are well over half of the way to the summit and the prospect ahead always seems more daunting than it is difficult. It still has this effect on me even some 60 ascents later.)

It was 15 years later before I returned to the great glen under Donard, this time serving a labouring apprenticeship as a trainee forester. My squad spent six winter months fencing in the north slope of the valley and across the face of Slievenamaddy, to keep the sheep and rabbits out, and planting the

We made that – the Glen River valley's somewhat patchy forest garb

thousands of noble and giant fir and Lodgepole pine that now clothe them – retreating to more sheltered activities in the lower forest when the ground froze too hard to put a spade into it or the blast of Donard's breath threatened to blow our saplings back out of it.

Circumstances cut short a forestry life and it was another 15 years before I returned to the Mournes – to a baptism of agonies, having been talked into taking part in a great populist event of that time – the yearly Mourne Wall Walk. Twenty two miles long with some 10,000 uphill feet to be climbed – for an inadequately prepared mountain novice it was 11 hours of 'challenge' and then some.

But in some way it was that day that opened my eyes to the lure of the mountain world that I had missed out on through the years – and the physical grief it gave me also made me aware of the entry fee it would demand in terms of fitness and new skills. The Mournes themselves provided the first and the second came from experience and week-ends of great crack with Teddy Hawkins's staff and the volunteers of the Tollymore Mountain Centre, which is now Northern Ireland's national Centre for Outdoor Activities. Over the next few years I learned the names and ways and moods of the mountains and how to 'survive' their vagaries (and my own misjudgements).

The Mourne Wall Walk itself was a case history in environmental short-sightedness. It became an annual event for myself but five years later a halt was called to it when in its Jubilee Year appalling weather and excessive numbers turned it into a disastrous 22-mile squelch. It caused unprecedented new levels of damage to the vegetation along the route, adding to what had been allowed to grow over the years in spite of the warnings and pleas, and eventually action, for an end to such events by people of awareness such as Dawson Stelfox and his friends in a new young climbing fraternity.

Even now, nearly 20 years on, slow-to-heal scars remain a silent reproach to those of us who didn't stop and think – or rather didn't think, and stop.

MOURNE MILLENNIUM

LIKE GLOW worms on the march, a long chain of flickering torchlights moved through the darkness far below, some single, others in little clusters, as people who had come from far and wide made their way up the Glen River track to be in the only place they regarded as fitting to experience a unique event. They were people to whom the Mournes gave much and to whom their highest summit was the natural place from which to witness the dawning of a new millennium.

Some would have restrained themselves in the more traditional forms of celebration a few hours before, saving themselves for the climb, others probably found their feet had wings with the lingering effects of their earlier celebrations! But whatever their state, in ones or twos they crunched their way up the frozen slopes until there were 60, maybe 70, of them waiting for the sliver of light on the eastern horizon that would open a new era.

In an inspired gesture one woman made the climb with a large rocket projecting from her haversack; propped it among the stones of Donard's summit cairn and at sunrise sent it soaring into the painted sky – a greeting to the new millennium from the mountains and those who walk them.

Some years you and Donard alone might wait the rising of the first sun of a new year, sometimes there would be a few others to share it. If you are lucky maybe one time in three you might actually have a clear sky to see a sunrise! For man's millennium

however, the weather was so perfect, with just a few ribbons of high cloud to glow in the brightening sky, it seemed as if nature and the mountains themselves were celebrating too.

To the mountains millennia are as days are to man. What manner of people, thirty generations hence, will climb to Donard's summit for the dawning of the next millennium?

A new millennium dawns in Mourne.

'Epilogue'

These are my riches, that none can take
    away from me,
Stored as mountain-grass is stored in the
    byre;
These shall shine on an evening when
    winter befalls me,
Sitting by the fire.

Mine are the torrents and the timeless hills,
The rock-face and the heather and the rain,
The summits where the life-wind thrums
    and thrills,
And, answering, the glad heart sings again:
The good grey rock that loves the
    grasping hand,
The stress of body, and the soul's rebirth
On the tall peaks where gods and men may
    stand
Breathless above the kingdoms of the earth.

The drowse of summer on the sunlit crags,
Lulled in the blue and shimmering air of
    June,
When time, the lazy mountain traveller,
    lags
To dream with us an endless afternoon:
The ice-wind stealing downwards from the
    crest
To hush with frost the reedy river's flow,
When all the mountain-land on winter's
    breast
Sleeps in the deathly silence of the snow.

These are my riches, these and the bright
    remembering
Of ridge and buttress and sky-shouldering
    spire;
These I shall count, when I am old, of an
    evening,
Sitting by the fire.

SHOWELL STYLES

WHY IS IT CALLED THAT?

Altataggart – Height of the Priest (where
    clandestine Mass was said in penal times)

Ben Crom – The curved peak
Butter Mountain – From booleying times

Carn – Mountain of the Cairn
Clonachullion – The river-side meadow where holly
    trees grow
Cock Mountain and Hen Mountain – Originally
    regarded, more logically, as a single mountain,
    named 'Cock and Hen'
Cove Mountain – Cove as in 'sheltered bay',
    referring to the plateau containing Cove Lough
Crossone – Place of the river crossing
Crotlieve – Hump-backed Mountain

Doan – The citadel

Finlieve – White Mountain
Formal – Round Hill

Knockchree – Hill of the Cattle
Knockshee – Fairy Hill

Leganabruchan – The rocks of the badgers
Legawherry – The rocky cauldron
Leckanmore – The big hillside of the slabs

Moneyscalp – The wooded chasm
Moughanmore – A great booley place

Ott – The breast of the hill

Poullaphuca – The Lair of the Goblin
Pulgarve – Rough hollow

Roosley – Possibly Red Hill but probably a family
    name

Seefin – Suidhe Finn – Finn's resting place (Finn
    MacCumhail)
Shanlieve and Shanslieve – Old Mountain
Shannagh (Lough) – Lake of the Foxes
Shimna – River of the Rushes, a more romantic
    (19th century) name for the river previously
    called Hanalock – Abha-na-lag – River of the
    Deep Pools
Slieveban – White Mountain
Slieve Bearnagh – Gapped Mountain (the saddle
    between its tors)
Slieve Binnian – Mountain of the Sharp Peaks
    (the tors)
Slieve Commedagh – Mountain of the Watching
Slieve Corragh – Rugged Mountain
Slieve Donard – After the saint
Slievefadda – Long mountain ridge
Slieve Lamagan – Creeping Mountain, i.e. a hands
    as well as feet ascent!
Slievemageogh – Mageogh's Mountain (from the
    MacEochys, the resettled Mughdhorna
    [Mourne] clan from Monaghan who gave the
    region their name)
Slieve Meelbeg – Lesser bald or smooth-topped
    mountain (i.e. without tors)
Slieve Meelmore – Greater bald mountain (actually
    lower than Meelbeg but appears higher)

Slievemeen – Mountain with Meadows

Slieve Muck – Muc – Mountain of the Pigs

Slievenabrock – Badger Mountain

Slievenagarragh – Mountain of the Rough Fields

Slievenaglogh (three of them!) – Stony Mountain

Slievenagore – Mountain of Goats

Slievenamaddy – Mountain of Dogs

Slievenaman (na mban) – The Mountain of the (fairy) Women

Slievenamiskan – The Mountain of the Butter (storage) Vessel

Slieveroe – Red Mountain (two of them)

Spelga and Spellack – Splintered rocks

Tornam(b)rock – Peak of the Badgers

Tievedockaragh – The Rough Hillside

Trassey – The fierce (river)

Tullymore – The Great Hill

Slieve Lamagan – the Creeping Mountain!

WANT TO KNOW MORE?

MANY STUDIES have been carried out on different aspects of the natural history of the Mournes and many people have recorded their personal experiences of them, especially in the second half of the nineteenth century.

The following is not a definitive list of publications but will lead down many paths of interest for those wanting to pursue more detailed knowledge. Some deal specifically with the Mournes, others in general with subjects, such as geology and past climates, botany and man's early life in Ireland, which are the background against which their story is written.

Some of the books are available now only from the more comprehensive local library collections, such as that of the most excellent Linen Hall Library in Belfast. The Queen's University science libraries contain some interesting papers as do the proceedings of the Belfast Naturalists Field Club. Belfast Geologists' Society numbers among its members the leading experts on the formation and development of the mountain landscape.

The Masterclass works
Mourne Country – Estyn Evans (Dundalgen Press, 1951)
Shell Guide to Reading the Irish Landscape – Frank Mitchell (Michael Joseph/Country House, 1986)

Geology
Regional Geology of Northern Ireland – Geological Survey for Northern Ireland, 1972
A Story Through Time – Patrick McKeever (Landscapes from Stone) – Geological Survey for Northern Ireland, 1999
A Geology of Ireland – C H Holland (Edit) (Scottish Academic Press, 1981)
Geology and Scenery in Ireland – J B Whittow (Pelican Books, 1974)
Field Excursion Guide to the Tertiary Volcanic Rocks of Ireland – Emeleus and Preston (1969)

Archaeology and history
The Archaeology of Ulster – Mallory and McNeill (Institute of Irish Studies, QUB, 1991)
The Environment of Early Man in the British Isles – John G Evans (Paul Eleck, 1975)
Pre-Christian Ireland – Peter Harbison (Thames & Hudson)
Ordnance Survey Memoirs of Ireland 1834-6 (South Down) (Institute of Irish Studies, QUB, 1990)
Victorian and Edwardian Newcastle – Grenfell Morgan (Friar's Bush Press, 1988)
The Dam Builders – The Story of the Men who Built The Mourne Wall and the Silent Valley Reservoir – W H Carson (Mourne Observer Press, 1974)
Place Names of Northern Ireland, Volume 3, 'The Mournes' (Ed. Gerard Stockman) (Institute of Irish Studies, QUB, 1993)
'Early Settlers of Mourne' – Alison Sheridan – Feature in *Twelve Miles of Mourne*, 1989 (The Journal of the Mourne Local Studies Group)

Natural History
Nature in its Place – Stephen Mills – (Bodley Head/RTE, 1988)
Bellamy's Ireland – The Wild Boglands – David Bellamy (Country House, 1986)

Mountains and Moorlands – W H Pearsall (Collins New Naturalist Series, 1971)

'Changing Vegetation of the Mournes' – Kenneth Hirons – *Twelve Miles of Mourne* (1988)

Upland Birdlife in the Mournes – Anthony McGeehan – ditto (1991)

'Botany of the Mourne Mountains' – Stewart & Praeger (Paper to Royal Irish Academy, 1892)

'The Ecology of the Mountains of Mourne with Special Reference to Slieve Donard' – Paper by Armstrong, Calvert and Ingold – Queen's University 1930

A full botanical list from a recent survey of Mourne upland plants is available from the Mourne Heritage Trust.

Useful guides for plant identification

Collins Guides to the Wild Flowers and to the Grasses, Sedges, Rushes and Ferns of Britain and Northern Europe (1996) (The ones to pack)

Grasses, Ferns, Mosses and Lichens of Britain – Roger Phillips (Pan Books, 1980)

Walk selections

Bernard Davey's Mourne -two volumes (Cottage Publications, 1999; 2001)

The Mournes – Walks – Excellently detailed and informative descriptions of 32 high and low level walks by Paddy Dillon (O'Brien Press, 2000)

Irish Peaks – Joss Lynam (Constable, 1982)

Irish Walk Guides (North East) – Richard Rogers (Gill & Macmillan, 1980)

Hill Walks in the Mournes – J S Doran (Mourne Observer Press)

Mourne Mountain Walks – A series of individual walk cards – Mourne Heritage Trust

. . . accompanied always of course by the essential companions, the Mourne Country Outdoor Pursuits Map (1:25,000 scale produced by the Ordnance Survey of Northern Ireland) – and your compass!

Personal and descriptive writings

The Way That I Went – Robert Lloyd Praeger (The Collins Press, Cork, republished 1999)

The Mournes – Colin Turner and Niki Hill (Cottage Publications, 1997)

An Echo in Another's Mind – Bert Slader (Quest Books (NI), 1994)

Speak to the Hills – an Anthology of Twentieth Century British and Irish Mountain Poetry Edited by Hamish Brown, Martyn Berry & Norman Nicholson (Aberdeen University Press, 1987)

Other books and brochures now out of print

Official Guide to County Down – Robert Lloyd Praeger (1900) (Still one of the best ever guides to the Mournes)

The Botanist in Ireland – Robert Lloyd Praeger (1934)

Legendary Stories of the Carlingford Lough District – Michael George Crawford of Warrenpoint (V G Havern, Warrenpoint)

Beatty's guide to Newcastle and Vicinity (1906)

South Armagh, Newry and the Mourne Mountains – S W Chambers (1941) (A guide for the forces stationed in Northern Ireland during the War)

The Ordnance Survey Letters of John O'Donovan (1834)

The Antient and Present State of the County of Down by Walter Harris (1744)

An Historical Account of the Diocese of Down and Connor by the Rev. James O'Laverty (1878)

Letters from Ireland by Charlotte Elizabeth (1859)

Travels in Ireland (1840) – Mr & Mrs Hall

Tours in Ulster – J B Doyle (1854)

In Search of Ireland – H V Morton (1937)

'Apollo in Mourne' – anthology of verse by Richard Rowley edited by Victor Price (Blackstaff Press, 1983)

Round Mourne – J W Montgomery (1908)

The Mountains of Mourne; Their Charm, and Their People – Louise McKay (Jarrolds Publishers, 1837)

The Mourne Heritage Trust

THE MOURNE Heritage Trust is the body responsible for the environmental management of the Mourne Area of Outstanding Natural Beauty – as well as driving a wide range of rural regeneration, cultural heritage and amenity development programmes.

Although Mourne AONB is dominated by the Mountains of Mourne, it covers a much wider area of 'living landscape', stretching from Carlingford Lough in the south to Slieve Croob in the north and including a kaleidoscope of mountain, coastal, forest and agricultural environments.

The Mourne Heritage Trust board is representative of all organisations with an interest in and a contribution to make to the well-being and future development of the area and its communities, ranging from statutory bodies to environmental interests and visitor facility providers.

The wider public can share in the Trust's practical work of protecting the mountain environment through participation in projects of the Mourne Conservation Volunteers and membership of The Friends of Mourne can give individuals an opportunity to support its work and a voice in the development of its policies.

The Trust also organises guided mountain walks during the summer led by staff rangers and its staff can provide advice and guidance for visitors.

The Trust is based at:

The Countryside Centre,
87 Central Promenade,
Newcastle, Co Down,
BT33 0HH
Telephone 028 4372 4059
Email: mht@mourne.co.uk

Advice, a range of maps, walking routes and other publications are all available.

INDEX

Index compiled by Paul Harron

ACKNOWLEDGEMENTS

MY THANKS are due first to Appletree Press for its support and commitment in bringing this work to fruition, and especially to Paul Harron for his tactful guidance, hard work and tolerance. Special thanks are due to Dawson Stelfox for his thoughtful foreword and I am grateful to Dr Arthur Mitchell of Mourne Heritage Trust for his valuable suggestions, and to Sandra Newell of Glassdrumman for her wealth of helpful information. As always, the Linen Hall Library in Belfast proved a never-failing source of knowledge.

The Robert Welch photograph on page 110 and John Luke's painting *In the Mournes* on page 66 are reproduced with the kind permission of the Trustees of the National Museums & Galleries of Northern Ireland. I am grateful to Mrs Sarah McKee for granting copyright permission to include the Luke work.

My thanks to Mr Michael Williams for permission to use the incomparable poems of his father 'Richard Rowley' and to the Northern Ireland Mountain Training Board for the articles by Brian Gibson, Freddie McCann and Teddy Hawkins. My thanks are also due to Ruth Bidgood for permission to print her poem 'Stone'. Other authors quoted include: Estyn Evans (*Mourne Country*) – Dundalgen Press, Dundalk; J S Doran (*My Mourne*) and W H Carson (*The Dam Builders*) – both Mourne Observer Press; Michael George Crawford – 'Lough Shannagh's Sprite' (*Legendary Stories of the Carlingford Lough District*) – VG Havern, Warrenpoint; and Robert Lloyd Praeger (*The Way That I Went*) – The Collins Press, Cork.

The following poems have been sourced from *Speak to the Hills – an Anthology of Twentieth Century British and Irish Mountain Poetry* edited by Hamish Brown, Martyn Berry and Norman Nicholson and published by Aberdeen University Press – 'On the Plateau' by Eilidh Nisbet, 'Great Mountains Love Great Storms' by Geoffrey Winthrop Young, 'The Rune and the Echo' and 'Mountain Burn' by Brenda Macrow, 'Rock' by Keith Battarbee, 'Epilogue' by Showell Styles and 'The Goat of Slieve Donard' by Patrick Kavanagh. 'Ireland' by W R Rodgers is sourced from *Awake and other Poems* published by Martin Secker.

Every effort has been made to trace copyright holders of all the works but where this has proved impossible and a work has been included in the anthology I trust that its use in this context will be approved and welcomed; any oversights will be rectified at the first opportunity.